Guiding Thos

In Massachusetts

2nd Edition

LEGAL AND PRACTICAL THINGS
YOU NEED TO DO
TO SETTLE AN ESTATE IN MASSACHUSETTS

and

HOW TO ARRANGE YOUR OWN AFFAIRS
TO AVOID UNNECESSARY COSTS
TO YOUR FAMILY

By AMELIA E. POHL, ESQ.

and Massachusetts Attorney
ROBERT J. REDDY

 EAGLE PUBLISHING COMPANY OF BOCA

The purpose of this book is to provide the reader with an informative overview of the subject; but laws change frequently and are subject to different interpretations as courts rule on the meaning or effect of a law. This book is sold with the understanding that neither the authors, nor the editors, nor the publisher, nor the distributors of this book are engaging in, or rendering, legal, accounting, financial planning, medical, or any other professional service. If you need legal, accounting, medical, financial planning or any other expert advice, then you should seek the services of a licensed professional.

This book is intended for use by the consumer for his or her own benefit. If you use this book to counsel someone about the law or tax matters, then that may be considered to be an unauthorized and illegal practice.

WEB SITES: Web sites appear throughout the book. These Web sites are offered for the convenience of the reader only. Publication of these Web site addresses is not an endorsement by the authors, editors or publishers of this book.

EAGLE PUBLISHING COMPANY OF BOCA
4199 N. Dixie Highway, #2
Boca Raton, FL   33431   E-mail: info@eaglepublishing.com

Printed in the United States of America
ISBN 1-892407-50-7
Library of Congress Catalog Card Number: 00-1150545

ii

Guiding Those Left Behind
In Massachusetts

2nd Edition

CONTENTS

About The Book

We tried to make this book as comprehensive as possible so there are specialized sections of the book that do not apply to the general population and may not be of interest to you. The following GUIDE POSTS appear throughout the book. You can read the section if the situation applies to you or skip the section if it doesn't. Skipping the section will not affect the continuity of the book.

GUIDE POSTS

The SPOUSE POST means that the information provided is specifically for the spouse of the decedent. If the decedent was single, you can skip this section.

The CALL-A-LAWYER POST alerts you to a situation that may require the assistance of an attorney. See the end of this chapter for information about how to find a lawyer.

The CAUTION POST alerts you to a potential problem. It is followed by a suggestion about how to avoid the problem.

The SPECIAL SITUATION POST means that the information given in that paragraph applies to a particular event or situation; for example when the decedent dies a violent death. If the situation does not apply, you can skip the section.

The Organization of the Book

Guiding Those Left Behind refers to the things that need to be done in order to settle an Estate in Massachusetts. The purpose of this book is to guide the reader through that process. It explains:

1. How to tend to the funeral and burial
2. What agencies need to be notified
3. How to locate the decedent's property
4. What bills need (and do not need) to be paid
5. How to determine who is entitled to inherit the decedent's property
6. How to transfer the decedent's property to the proper beneficiary

We devoted a chapter to each of these 6 steps; and for those who in charge of settling an Estate, we placed a CHECK LIST at the end of Chapter 6 summarizing those need to be done. Once you read Chapters 1 through 6 you will be able to identify those problems that can happen when someone dies. Using those Chapters as a base, you can set up your own Estate Plan so that your family is not burdened by similar problems. The rest of the book (Chapters 7, 8 and 9) suggests different methods you can use to accomplish this goal.

GLOSSARY

This book is designed for the average reader. Legal terminology has been kept to a minimum. There is a glossary at the end of the book in the event you come across a legal term that is not familiar to you.

FICTITIOUS NAMES AND EVENTS

The examples in this book are based loosely on actual events; however, all names are fictitious; and the events, as portrayed, are fictitious.

Reading the Law

Where applicable, we identified the state statute or federal statute that is the basis of the discussion. We did this as a reference, and also to encourage the general public to read the law as it is written. Prior to the Internet the only way you could look up the law was to physically take yourself to the local courthouse law library or the law section of a public library. Today all of the state and federal statutes are literally at your finger tips. They are just a mouse click away on the Internet.

To look up the law all you need is the address of the Web site and the identifying number of the statute.

    FEDERAL STATUTES
http://www4.law.cornell.edu/uscode

MASSACHUSETTS STATUTES
http://www.state.ma.us/legis/

Massachusetts laws are organized into some 282 chapters. Each chapter is further divided into sections. We have identified the Massachusetts law by Chapter and section. For example (MGL 112:84) refers to the Massachusetts General Laws, Chapter 112, Section 84.

To look up a statute, all you need do is go to the Web site, find the Chapter and then the section within that Chapter.

For those topics that are important to you, you may find it both interesting and profitable to read the law as it is

Robert J. Reddy, Esq.

ROBERT J. REDDY graduated from the New England School of Law in 1982. He is a Certified Financial Planner ("CFP"), Chartered Financial Consultant ("ChFC") and Certified Life Underwriter ("CLU"). He maintains memberships in the American Bar Association, the Massachusetts Bar Association, the Barnstable Bar Association and the National Academy of Elder Law Attorneys. Mr. Reddy has held several positions and chairmanships in professional and civic organizations and in past years was active in local politics and in several Veterans' organizations.

Attorney Reddy, is a man of many talents. He enjoyed a twenty year naval career, living for extended periods of time in Italy, Iceland, Iran, Germany, Bermuda and the Antarctic. He has had an interest in writing that goes back many years. He has had several articles published in professional journals and newspapers, and has written two books: *2500 Q and A on Naval Military Subjects* and *500 Part/Full Time Money-Making Opportunities*

Reddy's legal practice is unique on Cape Cod. He is an attorney and also a Certified Financial Planner, and a fully licensed securities broker. By combining his legal expertise with his extensive background as a Certified Financial Planner, he is able to provide a full range of services for the continuing needs of his clients.

While maintaining a full time legal practice, Mr. Reddy also gives seminars on legal matters and financial planning. Having given over 400 seminars throughout his professional career, Mr. Reddy is much demand as a public speaker. He also taught courses for the CFP program in the areas of Estate Planning, taxation and insurance for Northeastern University. He has taught a number of insurance courses to insurance professionals, as well.

Mr. Reddy concentrates his law practice in the areas of Estate Planning, Estate Administration, Probate and Elder Law. His clientele represents a broad economic background from the small business person to clients needing advice on the protection of multimillion dollar estates.

Bob Reddy and his wife Barbara, moved to Cape Code twenty-four years ago with their nine children who are now spread across the country, mostly on the East Coast. The family now includes a total of nineteen grandchildren. Unfortunately, Barbara Reddy passed away in April, 2000.

You can learn more about Mr. Reddy at his Web site:
http://www.robertreddy.com
E-mail address: bobreaddy@gis.net

Amelia E. Pohl, Esq.

Before becoming an attorney in 1985, AMELIA E. POHL taught mathematics on both the high school and college level. During her tenure as Associate Professor of Mathematics at Prince George's Community College in Maryland, she wrote several books including

Probability: A Set Theory Approach
Principals of Counting
Common Stock Sense.

During her practice of law Attorney Pohl observed that many people want to reduce the high cost of legal fees by performing or assisting with their own legal transactions. Attorney Pohl found that, with a bit of guidance, people are able to perform many legal transactions for themselves. Attorney Pohl utilizes her background as teacher, author and attorney to provide that "bit of guidance" to the general public in the form of self-help legal books that she has written. Amelia E. Pohl is currently "translating" this book for the remaining 49 states:

Guiding Those Left Behind in Maine
Guiding Those Left Behind In North Dakota
Guiding Those Left Behind In Wyoming, etc.

THE DESIGN ARTIST
LUBOSH CECH designed the cover of this book. He is a renowned artist, with extensive educational background and professional work experience. He studied design, applied art, and painting in his native Prague, Czech Republic. Just before graduating from the Ph.D. program in art history at the Charles University in Prague, he defected to Italy to escape the political persecution of the communist government. While in Italy, he studied at the University of Bologna.

Since moving to the United States in 1984, Mr. Cech has been designing art exhibitions, working as an art director, and graphic designer. Mr. Cech is a photographer and often incorporates his photographs into his art work.

Lubosh Cech is the founder of OKO DESIGN STUDIO located in Portland, Oregon. He designs promotional materials for print and digital media. He has received numerous rewards for both graphic design and painting. For more information about Mr. Cech and the OKO Design Studio visit his Web site.
http://www.okodesignstudio.com

THE PHOTOGRAPHER
The photograph that appears on the cover was taken by photographer GENE OSON.

ACKNOWLEDGMENT

When someone dies, the family attorney is often among the first to be called. Family members have questions about whether probate is necessary, who to notify, how to get possession of the assets, etc. Over the years, as we practiced in the field of Elder Law, we noticed that the questions raised were much the same family to family. We both agreed that a book answering such questions would be of service to the general public.

We also observed, that those who had experience in settling the estate of a loved one were more understanding of the process, and better able to make decisions about how to arrange their own finances to avoid problems that could arise in settling an estate. We named the book *Guiding Those Left Behind*. The "Guiding" refers to the guidance that this book gives in the event that you need to settle the Estate of your loved one. It also refers to the guidance that you can give to your family by setting up your own Estate Plan so that your family is not burdened by unnecessary costs and delays in settling your estate.

We wish to thank all of the clients, whom we have had the honor and pleasure to serve, for providing us with the impetus to produce this book.

When You Need A Lawyer

The purpose of this book is to give the reader a basic understanding of Massachusetts law as it relates to Wills and other methods of Estate Planning. It is not intended as a substitute for legal counsel or any other kind of professional advice. If you have any legal question, you should seek the counsel of an attorney. When looking for an attorney, consider three things:
EXPERTISE, COST and PERSONALITY.

EXPERTISE

The state of Massachusetts does not have a program to certify that an attorney is specialized in a particular area of law. This being the case an attorney in Massachusetts may not represent to the public that he/she is certified by the state as a specialist in any given area of law. Attorneys are allowed to state that they concentrate on certain areas of law or that they limit their practice to an area of law.

The Lawyer Referral Service is a public service program of the Massachusetts State Bar Association. They can refer you to an attorney in your area that practices in the type of law that you seek. The cost of the initial half hour consultation is currently no more than $25.

Within Massachusetts, you can reach the Lawyer Referral Service at (800) 392-6164. Out of state call (617) 338-0500. The Massachusetts Bar Association has a Web site with a list of Lawyer Referral Services throughout the state.

 THE MASSACHUSETTS BAR ASSOCIATION
http://www.massbar.org/

One of the most reliable ways of finding an attorney is through personal referral. Ask your friends, family or business acquaintances if they used an attorney for the field of law that you seek and whether they were pleased with the results. It is important to employ an attorney who is experienced in the area of law you seek. Your friend may have a wonderful Estate Planning attorney, but if you suffered an injury to your body, you need an attorney who is experienced in Personal Injury.

Before employing an attorney for a job, ask how long he has practiced that type of law and what percentage of his practice is devoted to that type of law.

COST

In addition to the attorney's experience, it is important that you check out what you can expect to pay in attorney's fees. When you call for an appointment ask what the attorney will charge for the initial consultation and the approximate cost for the service you seek. Ask whether there will be any additional costs such as filing fees, accounting fees, expert witness fees, etc.

If the least expensive attorney is out of your price range then there are many state and private agencies throughout the state that provide legal assistance for people of low income. You can call your local county Bar Association for the telephone number of the agency nearest you.

The American Bar Association has a list of Massachusetts Legal Services Programs at the <u>General Public Resources</u> section of its Web site.

 AMERICAN BAR ASSOCIATION
http://www.abanet.org

PERSONALITY

Of equal importance to the attorney's experience and legal fees, is your relationship with the attorney. How easy was it to reach the attorney? Did you go through layers of receptionists and legal assistants before being allowed to speak to the attorney? Did the attorney promptly return your call? If you had difficulty reaching the attorney, then you can expect similar problems should you employ that attorney.

Did the attorney treat you with respect? Did the attorney treat you paternally with a "father knows best" attitude or did he treat you as an intelligent person with the ability to understand the options available to you and the ability to make your own decision based on the information provided to you?

Are you able to understand and easily communicate with the attorney? Is he speaking to you in plain English or is his explanation of the matter so full of legalese to be almost meaningless to you?

Do you find the attorney's personality to be pleasant or grating? Sometimes people rub each other the wrong way. It is like rubbing a cat the wrong way. Stroking a cat from head to tail is pleasing to the cat, but petting it in the opposite direction, no matter how well intended, causes friction. If the lawyer makes you feel annoyed or uncomfortable, then find another attorney.

It is worth the effort to take the time to interview as many attorneys as it takes to find one with the right expertise, fee schedule and personality for you.

The First Week 1

Dealing with the death of a close family member or friend is difficult. Not only do you need to deal with your own emotions, but often with those of your family and friends. Sometimes their sorrow is more painful to you, than what you are experiencing yourself.

In addition to the emotional impact of a death, there are many things that need to be done, from arranging the funeral and burial, to closing out the business affairs of the *decedent* (the person who died) and finally giving whatever property is left to the proper beneficiary.

The funeral and burial take only a few days. Wrapping up the affairs of the decedent may take considerably longer. This chapter explains what things you (the spouse or closest family member) need to do during the first week, beginning at the moment of death and continuing through the funeral.

  MALE GENDER USED

Rather than use "he/she" or "his/her" for simplicity
(and hoping not to offend anyone)
we will refer to the decedent and his
Personal Representative using the male gender.

References to other people will be in both genders.

AUTOPSIES

In today's high tech world of medicine, doctors are fairly certain of the cause of death, but if there is a question as to the cause of death, the family should consider having an autopsy performed. The person giving authorization must agree to pay for the autopsy because the cost is not covered under most health insurance plans.

The cost of an autopsy can run anywhere from several hundred to several thousand dollars, but it is in the family's best interest to consent to the autopsy. The examination might reveal a genetic disorder that could be treated if it later appears in another family member. Death from a car "accident" could have been a heart attack at the wheel. Perhaps the patient who died suddenly in a hospital was misdiagnosed. The nursing home resident could have died from negligence and not old age. Even if none of these are found, knowing the cause of death with certainty is better than not knowing.

That was the case with the family of a woman who was taken to the hospital complaining of stomach pains. The doctors thought she might be suffering from gallbladder disease but she died before they could effectively treat her. A doctor suggested that an autopsy be performed to determine the actual cause of death. The woman had three daughters, one of whom objected to the autopsy: "Why spend that kind of money? It won't bring Mom back."

The daughter's wishes were respected, however over the years as they aged and became ill with their own various ailments, they would undergo physical examinations. As part of taking their medical history, doctors routinely asked "And what was the cause of your mother's death?" None could answer the question.

This is not a dramatic story. No mysterious genetic disorder ever occurred in any of her daughters, nor in any of their children. But each daughter (including the one who objected) at some point in her life, was confronted with the nagging question "What did Mom die of?"

MANDATORY AUTOPSIES

When a person dies, a physician or a registered nurse must sign the death certificate stating the cause of death. If a person dies in a hospital, then there is someone present to sign the certificate. If a person dies at home from natural causes and is under the care of a registered nurse from Hospice, then the physician or the registered nurse can sign the death certificate and the funeral director can take possession of the body. In such case, there is no need to call 911. But if a person discovers a body of a person who was not under the care of a physician, or who died suddenly either from illness, accident, suicide or foul play, then the police must be summoned. The police will ask the County Medical Examiner to determine the cause of death. The Medical Examiner or the District Attorney will order an autopsy whenever there is a suspicion that the death was not from natural causes or that the death was caused by a disease that could pose a threat to the public health (MGL 38:4).

AUTOPSIES PERFORMED BY THE INSURANCE COMPANY
It may be that the decedent had an accident and sickness insurance policies that contains a provision giving the insurance company the right to perform an autopsy. If the decedent had such a policy and the death occurred under circumstances that warrant investigation, then the insurance company may order an autopsy. The cost of the autopsy is paid for by the insurance company, so they will not order an autopsy unless there is some important reason to do so.

ANATOMICAL GIFTS

If, before death, the decedent made an anatomical gift by signing a donor card, then hospital personnel or the donor's doctor need to be made aware of the gift in quick proximity to the time of death — preferably before death.

GIFT AUTHORIZED BY THE FAMILY

Hospital personnel determine whether a mortally ill patient is a candidate for an organ donation. Early in the donor program those over 65 were not considered as suitable candidates. Today, however, the condition of the organ, and not the age, is the determining factor.

The federal government has established regional Organ Procurement Organizations throughout the United States to coordinate the donor program. The New England Organ Bank is the Organ Procurement Organization for Massachusetts and it is located in Newton, Massachusetts. If the hospital staff thinks that the patient is a candidate, the hospital will contact the New England Organ Bank. The Organ Bank will determine whether the patient is a suitable donor. If they decide to request the gift and the candidate did not sign a donor card then someone in the family must give written permission.

Massachusetts law establishes an order of priority to authorize the donation:
1st spouse   2nd an adult son or daughter
3rd either parent   4th an adult brother or sister
5th decedent's court appointed guardian (if any)
6th anyone else who is authorized to dispose of the body (MGL 113:8).

If permission is obtained from a family member and there If there are others in the same or a higher priority, then an effort must be made to contact those people and make them aware of the proposed gift. For example, if the brother of the decedent agrees to the gift (4th in priority). If permission is obtained from a family member and there are others in the same or a higher priority, then an effort must be made to contact those people and make them aware of the proposed gift. For example, if the sister of the decedent agrees to the gift (4th in priority) and the decedent had an adult child (2nd in priority), then the child needs to be made aware of the gift. If the child objects, then no gift can be made. Similarly, the statute prohibits the gift if the decedent ever expressed his opposition to a donation.

AFTER THE DONATION

Once the donation is made the body is delivered to the funeral home and prepared for burial or cremation as directed by the family. The donation does not disfigure the body so there can be an open casket viewing if the family so wishes.

Some regional Organ Procurement Organizations have an aftercare program that includes a letter of condolence to the family and an expression of gratitude for the gift. For privacy reasons, the identity of the recipient of the gift is not disclosed, but on request from the family, the local Organ Procurement Organization will give the family basic demographic information about the donation, such as the age, sex, marital status, number of children and occupation of the recipient of the gift.

GIFT FOR EDUCATION OR RESEARCH

Consider offering to release the body for the purpose of education or research in the event that the decedent signed a donor card, but was not an appropriate candidate for an organ donation. You can offer to release the body to any of the following institutions to be used for education or research:

University of Massachusetts
Anatomical Gifts Program
55 Lake Avenue North
Worchester, MA 01605
(508) 856-2460

Harvard Medical School
Anatomical Gifts Program
260 Longwood Avenue
Boston, MA 02115
(617) 432-1735

Tufts University
School of Medicine
Anatomical Gifts Program
136 Harrison Avenue
Boston, MA 02111
(617) 956-6685

Boston Univ. School of Medicine
Anatomical Gifts Program
80 East Concord Street
Boston, MA 02118
(617) 638-4245

You need to call the school to determine whether they will accept the body. Most schools will not accept bodies that have been autopsied or embalmed, or who are grossly obese. They will also refuse a donation from those who have died from a contagious disease or from crushing injuries. Schools usually pay for the local transportation of the body to the school and for the cost of obtaining the Burial/Removal Permit and a certified copy of the death certificate.

It takes up to two years to complete the study. Once the project is complete, the Harvard Medical School cremates the remains and return the ashes to the family. The University of Massachusetts, Tufts and Boston University School of Medicine do not cremate the remains but will either arrange for burial in the school cemetery or will return the body to the family for cremation or burial.

MAKING THE DONATION

In Massachusetts, an anatomical gift may be made to any hospital, physician, accredited medical or dental school, a bank or storage facility for the purpose of transplantation, education or research (MA 113:9). Federal law prohibits payment for organ donations (42 U.S.C. 274 e). There is no ban on payments made to prepare organs or tissue for transplantation, nor is there any ban on charges made to transport bodies or body parts. It is not legal for anyone to purchase body parts. Not-for profit as well as for-profit companies have sprung up that are in the business of preparing and delivering body parts. These companies request donations from families (so they are not buying body parts). The company prepares the body tissue or other parts of the body, and then distributes the parts throughout the United States to physicians, hospitals, research centers, etc. In many cases the monies charged for preparation and transportation includes a sizable profit. If someone other than the New England Organ Bank approaches you to make a donation, before agreeing to the donation you may want to learn about the company that is requesting the donation:

> What is their primary business activity?
> Where are their main headquarters located?
> What is the name and job description of the
> person making the request?

DETERMINE THE END USE OF THE DONATION

You may want to ask what they intend to do with the tissue or body part. If it is being used for research, then what type of research? Where is the research being conducted? If it will be used for transplantation, then what agency (doctor, hospital) will receive the donation and where is that agency located? Once you have this information you can make an informed decision as to whether you wish to make the donation to that company.

THE FUNERAL

Approximately ten percent of deaths occur suddenly because of accident, suicide, foul play or undetected illness. But, mostly, death occurs after a lengthy illness, with a common scenario being that of an aged person who dies after being ill for several months, if not years. In such case, family and friends are emotionally prepared for the happening. Expected or not, the first job is the disposition of the body.

THE PREARRANGED FUNERAL

Increasingly, people are arranging, in advance, for their own funeral and burial. This makes it easier on the family both financially and emotionally. All the decisions have been made and there is no guessing what the decedent would have wanted. If the decedent made provision for his burial, you should come across a burial certificate, or perhaps a deed to a burial space. If he made provision for his funeral, you should find a Pre-need funeral contract. Read the contract to determine what provisions were made. If the contract was paid by installment, find out whether it was paid in full. You also need to determine whether the contract was a fixed price agreement or whether there could be some additional charge.

If you cannot locate the contract, but you know the decedent made provision for his funeral, call the funeral home and ask them to send you a copy of the contract. If you believe the decedent purchased a funeral plan but you do not know the name of the funeral home, call the local funeral homes. Many local funeral homes are owned by national firms with computer capacity to identify people who have purchased a contract at any of their many locations.

Once you have possession of the contract, take it with you to the funeral home and go over the terms of the contract with the funeral director. Inquire whether there is any charge that is not included in the contract.

MAKING FUNERAL ARRANGEMENTS

If the decedent died unexpectedly or without having made any prior funeral arrangements then your first job is to choose a funeral director and make arrangements for the funeral or cremation. Most people choose the nearest or most conveniently located funeral home without comparison shopping. However prices for these services can vary significantly from funeral home to funeral home. Savings can be had if you take the time to make a few phone calls.

Receiving price quotes by telephone is your right under Federal law. Federal Trade Commission ("FTC") Rule 453.2 (b) (1) requires a funeral director to give an accurate telephone quote of the prices of his goods and services. Funeral homes are listed in the telephone directory under FUNERAL DIRECTORS. If you live in a small town, there may be only one or two listings. If such is the case, then check out some funeral homes in the next largest city.

Funeral directors usually provide the following services:
➢ arrange for the transportation of the body
   to the funeral home and then to the burial site
➢ obtain burial transit permits
➢ arrange for the embalming or cremation of the body
➢ arrange funeral and memorial services
   and the viewing of the body
➢ obtain information for the death certificate
➢ order copies of the death certificate for the family
➢ have memorial cards printed.

To compare prices you will need to determine:

✧ what is included in the price of a basic funeral plan

✧ whether you can expect any additional cost.

If the decedent did not own a burial space, then that cost must be included when making funeral arrangements.

It may be necessary to have the body embalmed if you are going to have a viewing. Embalming is not necessary if you order a direct cremation or an immediate burial without a viewing. Federal Trade Commission Rule 453.5 prohibits the funeral home from charging an embalming fee unless you order the service.

PURCHASING THE CASKET

When comparison-shopping, you will find that the single most expensive item to be a casket. When selecting a casket you need to be aware that there may be a considerable mark-up in the price quoted by the funeral director. You do not need to go "sole source" when purchasing the casket. If you feel that the price quoted by the funeral director is too high, you can purchase the casket elsewhere and have it delivered to the funeral home to be used instead of the one offered by the funeral director. Federal regulations require a funeral home to accept a casket that is purchased elsewhere.

The funeral director must provide you with a written price list at the beginning of your discussion of funeral arrangements. If the price list given to you by the funeral home states that the price of their casket includes a specific dollar amount for basic services, and you do not purchase the casket from the funeral home, then the funeral director is allowed to add that specific dollar amount to the charge for his basic services. He is not allowed to charge a handling fee for accepting a casket that is purchased elsewhere (FTC Rule 453.2, 453.4).

Of course the problem with purchasing a casket is that most of us have no idea what to pay. Caskets are not usually displayed for sale in a shopping mall, so how do you determine the going price? The answer is the Internet. You can learn all about the cost of any item, even a casket, by using your search engine to find a retail casket sales dealer. If you are not computer literate, you can locate the nearest retail casket sales outlet by looking in the yellow pages under CASKETS. You may need to look in the telephone directory for the nearest large city to find a listing. By making a call to a retail casket sales dealer, you will become knowledgeable in the price range of caskets. You can then decide what is a reasonable price for the product you seek.

The best time to do your comparison shopping is before you go to the funeral home to arrange for the funeral. Once you have determined what you should pay for the casket, it is only fair to give the funeral director the opportunity to meet that price. If you cannot reach a meeting of the minds, then you can always order the casket from the retail sales dealer and have it delivered to the funeral home.

ON-LINE FUNERAL SERVICES

The Internet is changing the way the world does business, and the funeral industry is no exception. A growing number of mortuaries are offering live Webcasts of funerals and wakes for those who are unable to pay their respects in person. There are Web sites where you can post an obituary. There are on-line memorial chat rooms as well as on-line eulogies and testimonials. There is even a Web site that offers a posthumous e-mail service which allows people to leave final messages for friends and relatives. You can locate these services using your favorite search engine and typing in "obituaries."

THE CREMATION

Increasingly people are opting for cremation. The reasons for choosing cremation are varied, but for the majority, it is a matter of finances. The cost of cremation is approximately one-sixth that of an ordinary funeral and burial. A major saving is the cost of the casket. No casket is necessary for the cremation. Federal law prohibits a funeral director from saying that a casket is required for a direct cremation (FTC Rule 453.3 (b)ii). If you wish to have a viewing or funeral service, you can arrange to rent a casket from the funeral director.

If you are not planning a viewing or funeral service prior to cremation, then consider contracting with a facility that does cremations only. Look in the telephone book under CREMATION SERVICES. You will also see cremation "societies" in the telephone book. Some are for-profit and others non-profit. You can also find advertisements for cremation services on the Internet.

THE OVERWEIGHT DECEDENT
If the decedent weighs more than 300 pounds, then you need to check to see if the cremation service has facilities large enough to handle the body. If you cannot locate a crematory that can accommodate the body, then you will need to make burial arrangements.

THE DECEDENT WITH A PACEMAKER
Cremating a body with a pacemaker or any radiation producing devise can cause damage to the cremation chamber or to the person performing the cremation. If the decedent was wearing such electronic aid, then you need to investigate the cost of having it removed prior to the cremation. The cremation service may be able help you to arrange for the removal of the device.

DISPOSING OF THE ASHES

The decedent's cremains can be placed in a cemetery. Many cemeteries have a separate building called a *columbarium*, which is especially designed to store urns. If not, the **cremains** (cremated remains) can be placed in a cemetery plot.

Some cemeteries allow the cremains of a family member to be placed in a occupied family plot. Similarly, some cemeteries will allow the cremains to be placed in the space in a mausoleum that is currently occupied by a member of the decedent's family. If you want to have the cremains placed in an occupied mausoleum or family plot, you need to call the cemetery and ask them to explain their policy as it relates to the burial of urns in occupied sites.

If the cremains are to be placed in a cemetery, then you need to obtain a suitable urn for the burial. You can purchase the urn from the funeral director or cremation service director. Urns cost much less than caskets, but they can cost several hundred dollars. You may wish to do some comparison shopping by calling a retail sales casket dealer.

SCATTERED AT SEA

The decedent may have expressed a desire to have his ashes placed at sea. The funeral director or cremation direction should be able to assist you in seeing to it that these wishes are respected. Federal law prohibits the ashes from being scattered any closer than three nautical miles from land, so you will need to arrange to have a boat carry the ashes out to sea (Code of Federal Regulations, Title 40, Section 229.1).

If the decedent is to be buried in another state, then the body will need to be transported to that state. Most funeral homes belong to a national network of funeral homes, and the out-of-state funeral director has the means to make local arrangements to ship the body. Contact the out-of-state funeral director and have him make arrangement with the airline for the transportation of the body.

If services are to be held in and in another state, then contact the local funeral director and he will make arrangements with the out-of-state funeral home for the transportation of the body.

If the body has been cremated, then you can transport the cremains yourself, either by carrying the ashes as part of your luggage or by arranging with the airline to transport the ashes as cargo. Have a certified copy of the death certificate available in the event that you need to identify the remains of the decedent. Call the airline before departure and ask whether they have any special regulation or procedure regarding the transportation of human ashes.

┃ SPOUSE ┃ THE MILITARY BURIAL

Subject to availability of burial spaces, an honorably discharged veteran and/or his unmarried minor or handicapped child and/or his un-remarried spouse may be buried in a national military cemetery. Some cemeteries have room only for cremated remains or for the casketed remains of a family member of someone who is currently buried in that cemetery, so you need to call for space availability.

There is one national military cemetery located in Massachusetts:

MASSACHUSETTS NATIONAL CEMETERY
Bourne, MA   02532

For information about burial there call (508) 563-7113.

ARLINGTON NATIONAL CEMETERY
The Department of the Army is in charge of the Arlington National Cemetery. If you wish to have an eligible deceased veteran buried in the Arlington National Cemetery, then call them at (703) 695-3250.

Arlington National Cemetery
Interment Service Branch
Arlington, VA 22211

THE COST OF A
MILITARY BURIAL

Burial space in a National Cemetery is free of charge. Cemetery employees will open and close the grave and mark it with headstone or grave marker without cost to the family. If requested, the local Veteran's Administration ("VA") will provide the family with a memorial flag. The VA will not pay to have the body transported to the cemetery, so the family needs to make transportation arrangements with a funeral firm.

Regardless of where an honorably discharged veteran is buried allowances may be available for the plot, and the burial and grave marker expenses. The amount varies depending on factors such as whether the veteran died because of a service related injury. The VA will not reimburse any burial or funeral expense for the spouse of a veteran.

For information about reimbursement of funeral and burial expenses you can call the VA at (800) 827-1000.

The Department of Veteran's Affairs has a Web site with information on the following topics:
> National and Military Cemeteries
> Burial, Headstones and Markers
> State Cemetery Grants Program
> Obtaining Military Records
> Locating Veterans

VA CEMETERY WEB SITE
http://www.cem.va.gov

BENEFITS FOR SPOUSE OF DECEDENT VETERAN

SPOUSE

The surviving spouse of an honorably discharged veteran should contact the Veteran's Administration to determine whether he/she is eligible for any benefits. For example, if the decedent had minor or disabled children, his spouse may also be eligible for a monthly benefit of Dependency and Indemnity Compensation ("DIC"). If the Veteran's surviving spouse receives nursing home care under Medicaid, then the spouse might be eligible for monthly payments from the VA.

Whether a surviving spouse is eligible for any of these benefits depends on many factors including whether the decedent was serving on active duty, whether his death was service related, and the surviving spouse's assets and income. DIC benefits are discontinued should the surviving spouse remarry; however, the law permits payments to be resumed in the event the new marriage ends because of death or divorce.

For information about whether the surviving spouse is eligible for any benefit related to the decedent's military service call the VA at (800) 827-1000. You can receive a printed statement of public policy: VA Pamphlet FEDERAL BENEFITS FOR VETERANS AND DE-PENDENTS by sending a check in the amount of $5 to
THE SUPERINTENDENT OF DOCUMENTS
P.O. Box 371954
Pittsburgh, PA 15250-7954
Information is also available at the VA Web site.

VETERAN'S ADMINISTRATION
http://www.va.gov

Each town in Massachusetts has at least one burial site. If an indigent person dies and the police know his identity, they will try to locate the family. If the identity of the decedent unknown, or if his family is unable or unwilling to arrange for his burial, then the officer of the township or municipal corporation where the body was found will have the body buried at public expense (MGL 114:10).

If the dean of a medical school has need of an anatomical gift for education or research, then the dean can submit a written application for a donation to the proper authority at any state support facility such as a penal institution or city hospital. Any body that is unclaimed, and must be buried at public expense, can be donated. The body will not be donated if the decedent is a veteran, or a stranger or traveler who died suddenly, or if prior to death the decedent asked for his body to be buried or delivered to a friend. Once the donation is made, the school is required to hold the body for 14 days to give friends or family of the decedent time to come forward and claim the body (MGL 113:1, 113:2, 113:3).

THE INDIGENT VETERAN

If the decedent was an honorably discharged veteran, then the family can arrange to have a Veteran's burial. If the police cannot locate the family of a deceased veteran, or if the veteran was indigent, the burial agent for the town or city, who will arrange for the burial. This service extends to the indigent decedent who was married to, or was a dependent of, a Veteran (MGL 115:7)

 **THE WRONGFUL DEATH**

If anyone committed a wrongful act against the decedent that led to his death, then regardless of whether that person is convicted of the crime, whoever is appointed by the Court to settle the Estate can sue for a wrongful death. Massachusetts law regulates who is entitled to the *damages* (payment from the wrongdoer); and in some cases, how much payment can be made. For example, the most that a city, town or county can be required to pay for a death caused by a defective railing on a roadway or a bridge is $4,000 (MGL 229:1).

WORK RELATED DEATH

The decedent's employer can be sued for a wrongful death if he or someone under his supervision, caused the death. If the death was not instantaneous and the decedent suffered prior to death, the wrongdoer can be sued for pain suffered by the decedent. Monies recovered for the death go to the surviving spouse, or if no spouse, to the next of kin who were dependent on the decedent for the support. Monies recovered for the conscious suffering become part of assets of the decedent's Estate to be distributed according to the Will or if he die without a Will, then according to the *Massachusetts Laws of Descent and Distribution* (see Chapter 5) (MGL 229:2, 229:2B, 229:6, 229:6C).

There are exceptions to the above statutes for certain deaths covered by the Workmen's Compensation Act, so it is important to consult with an attorney to examine all options which may be available to you

VICTIMS OF CRIME COMPENSATION PROGRAM

If the decedent died because of a criminal act and you are a family member, then you may be eligible to receive compensation under the MASSACHUSETTS COMPENSATION OF VICTIMS OF VIOLENT CRIMES LAW (MGL 258C). The state provides compensation for reasonable funeral expenses to $4,000) and/or medical expenses. Total compensation may not exceed $25,000. To be eligible the following must be true:

➢ The crime occurred in Massachusetts.

➢ The decedent was an innocent victim

➢ The crime was reported to authorities within 5 days of its commission or discovery of the body and the application for compensation filed within 3 years.

➢ There was full cooperation with law enforcement officers by the victim and/or his family.

To receive an application for compensation, you can call (617) 727-2200 or you can write to:

Division of Victim Compensation and Assistance
Office of the Attorney General
One Ashburton Place
Boston, MA 02108

Or you can download the application from the Internet.

 MASSACHUSETTS ATTORNEY GENERAL
http://www.ago.state.ma.us/

It usually takes from 4 to 6 months for the office to investigate and rule on your application.

THE PROBLEM
FUNERAL OR BURIAL

The funeral and burial industry is well regulated by both state and federal government. Under Massachusetts statute (MGL 112:84) the following acts are subject to disciplinary action:

⊠ Delivering goods of a lesser quality that presented to the purchaser as a sample

⊠ Using a false or misleading advertisement

⊠ gross immorality

⊠ using profane or obscene language in the presence of the decedent or within hearing of the family

⊠ Paying kick-backs to generate business

Funeral directors are licensed professionals so it is unusual to have a problem with the funeral or burial or cremation. However, if you had a bad experience with any aspect of the funeral then you can file a complaint with the state licensing agency:

Division of Registration of Funeral Services
239 Causeway Street
Boston, MA 02114
Telephone: (617) 727-1718

 **LAWYER**

In addition to filing a complaint with the Division of Registration of Funeral Services, you may wish to consult with an attorney who is experienced in litigation matters to learn of any other legal remedy that you may have.

THE MISSING BODY

Few things are more difficult to deal with than a missing person. The emotional turmoil created by the "not knowing" is often more difficult than the finality of death. The legal problems created by the disappearance are also more difficult than if the person simply died. It may take a two-part legal process — the appointment of a *Receiver* to manage the missing person's property, under Court supervison while he is missing, and then finally, a Probate procedure.

APPOINTING A RECEIVER

If a person is missing and cannot be found after a diligent search, then that person is referred to as an *absentee*. If the absentee has business matters that need attending (bills that need to be paid, checks that need to be cashed, etc.), the his spouse or next of kin can *petition* (ask) the Probate Court to appoint a Receiver until the person can be found. Before appointing a Receiver, the Court will require that a notice be published for three successive weeks giving the time and place of the hearing to appoint a Receiver. The notice will ask anyone who has an objection to appear at the hearing.

At the hearing the Court will determine the date of disappearance of the absentee. If a Receiver is not appointed, Probate can begin 6 years after the date of disappearance. If a Receiver is appointed, the Probate can begin one year after the appointment or after 7 years from the date of disappearance. Of course Probate can begin anytime there is sufficient evidence that the absentee is dead (MGL 200:3, 200:13).

THE DEATH CERTIFICATE

It is the job of the funeral director or cremation service director to provide information about the decedent to the Registry of Vital Records and Statistics. The office will prepare a death certificate based on that information. It is important that the information you give to the funeral or cremation director is correct. It is also important that you check the form completed by the funeral or cremation director to be sure names are correctly spelled and dates correctly written. Once the information is submitted to the Registry of Vital Statistics, it will be difficult and time consuming to make a correction.

The funeral or cremation director will order as many certified copies of the death certificate as you request. Most establishments require an original certified copy and not a photocopy so you need to order sufficient copies. The following is a list of institutions that may want a certified copy:

* Each insurance company that insured the decedent or his property (health, life, car insurance, etc.)
* Each financial institution in which the decedent had money invested (brokerage houses, banks)
* The decedent's pension fund
* Each credit card company used by the decedent
* The IRS
* The Social Security Administration
* The Registry of Motor Vehicles
* If a Probate procedure is necessary, then the Clerk of the Probate Court
* The Register of Deeds in each county where the decedent owned real property.

Some airlines and car rental companies offer a discount for short notice, emergency trips. If you have family flying in for the funeral, you may wish to order a few extra copies of the death certificate so that they can obtain an airline or car rental discount. If you wish to order certified copies of the death certificate at a later date, you can ask the funeral director to do so, or you can order copies yourself:

BY TELEPHONE
You can call the Registry of Vital Records at (617) 740-2606 and order the certificates using your credit card. The cost of a credit card order is $19.00 for the first certified copy and $14 for each additional copy of the same record.

AT THE REGISTRY
You can purchase a certified copy of the death certificate for $6 per copy at the Registry counter. They are open business days from 8:45-4:45 at the following address:

Registry of Vital Records and Statistics
150 Mount Vernon Street, 1st Floor
Dorchester, MA 02125-3105

BY MAIL
You can write to the Registry at the above address and they will forward a copy to you for $11 per copy. You should first call them at (617) 740-2600 and ask what information they require.

VIA THE INTERNET
You can order a certified copy via the Internet by going to the Department of Public Health section of the State of Massachusetts Web site. The cost for an Internet order is the same as a telephone order.

 MASSACHUSETTS — DEPT. OF PUBLIC HEALTH
http://www.state.ma.us/dph

About Probate

Once a person dies, all of the property he owns as of the date of his death is referred to as the **decedent's Estate.** If the decedent owned property that was in his name only (not jointly or in trust for someone) then some sort of Court procedure is necessary to determine who is entitled to possession of the property. The name of the Court procedure is **Probate**. We will use the term "Court" or "Probate Court" to refer to the judge who is presiding over Probate matters.

The root of the word Probate is "to prove." It refers to the first job of the Probate Court, that is, to examine proof of whether the decedent left a valid Will. The second job of the Probate Court is to appoint someone to wrap up the affairs of the decedent — to pay any outstanding bills and then to distribute what property is left to the proper beneficiary (MGL 215:6)

If the decedent left a valid Will naming someone to serve as *Executor* or *Personal Representative* or *Trustee* of his Estate, the Court will appoint that person for the job and issue *Letters Testamentary* giving him authority to administer the Estate. If the decedent died without a Will, the Court will appoint someone to be the *Administrator* of the his Estate and issue *Letters of Administration.*

For simplicity, we will refer to the person appointed by the Probate Court to settle the Estate as the decedent's **Personal Representative,** and the document authorizing him to act, as **Letters** (MGL 191B:12, 192:4).

There are different ways to conduct a Probate procedure depending on the value of the property that being Probated, and whether the decedent owned real property at the time of his death. We will refer to the property that is distributed as part of a Probate procedure as the decedent's **Probate Estate** and the method of conducting a Probate procedure as the **Estate administration**. Chapter 6 explains the different kinds of Estate administration that are available in the Commonwealth of Massachusetts.

But we are getting ahead of ourselves. First we need to determine whether a Probate procedure is necessary. To answer that question we need to know exactly what the decedent owned, so the next two chapters explain how to identify, and then locate, all of the decedent's assets.

Giving Notice Of The Death 2

Those closest to the decedent usually notify family members and close friends by telephone. The funeral director will arrange to have an obituary published in as many different newspapers as the family requests, but there is still the job of notifying the government and people who were doing business with the decedent. That task belongs to the person named as the Executor or Personal Representative of the decedent's Will.

In the absence of a valid Will, the spouse has the right to be appointed as Personal Representative. If there is no spouse, or if the spouse is unable or unwilling to serve, the next of kin have the right to be appointed (MGL 193:1). By *next of kin,* we mean those people who inherit the decedent's property according to the MASSACHUSETTS LAWS OF DESCENT. These laws are explained in Chapter 5.

If no Probate procedure is necessary, the job of notifying people of the death and settling the decedent's affairs falls to his spouse; and in the absence of a spouse, to the decedent's next of kin.

The person who has the job of settling the decedent's Estate should begin to give notice as soon as is practicable after the death. Two government agencies that need to be notified are the Social Security Administration and the IRS. This chapter gives their telephone number and other agencies that need to be notified.

NOTIFYING SOCIAL SECURITY

Many Funeral Directors will, as part of their service package, notify the Social Security Administration of the death. You may wish to check to see that this has been done. You can do so by calling (800) 772-1213. For the hearing impaired call (800) 325-0778 TTY. You will need to give the Social Security Administration the full legal name of the decedent as well as his social security number and date of birth.

| *Special Situation* | FOR DECEDENT RECEIVING SOCIAL SECURITY CHECKS |

If the decedent was receiving checks from Social Security, then you need to determine whether his last check needs to be returned to the Social Security Administration.

Each Social Security check is a payment for the prior month, provided that person lives for the entire prior month. If someone dies on the last day of the month, then you should not cash the check for that month. For example, if someone dies on July 31st, then you need to return the check that the agency mails out in August. If however, the decedent died on August 1st then the check sent in August need not be returned because that check is payment for the month of July.

If the Social Security check is electronically deposited into a bank account, then notify the bank that the account holder died and notify the Social Security Administration as well. If the check needs to be returned, then the Social Security Administration will withdraw it electronically from the bank account. You will need to keep the account open until the funds are withdrawn.

 **SPOUSE** | # THE SPOUSE AND CHILD'S SOCIAL SECURITY BENEFITS

If the decedent had sufficient work credits, the Social Security Administration will give the decedent's widow(er) or if unmarried, then the decedent's minor children, a one-time death benefit in the amount of $255.

SURVIVORS BENEFITS:

The spouse (or ex-spouse) of the decedent may be eligible for Survivors Benefits. Benefits vary depending on the amount of work credits earned by the decedent; whether the decedent had minor or disabled children; the spouse's age; how long they were married; etc. The decedent's minor child may be eligible for dependent child's benefits regardless of whether the decedent father ever married the child's mother. Paternity can be established by any one of several methods including the father acknowledging his child in writing or verbally to members of his family. For more information call the Social Security Administration at (800) 772-1213.

SOCIAL SECURITY BENEFITS

A spouse or ex-spouse can collect social security benefits based on the decedent's work record. This value may be greater than the spouse now receives. It is important to make an appointment with your local Social Security office and determine whether you as the spouse (or ex-spouse), or parent of the decedent's minor child, are eligible for Social Security or Survivor benefits. The Social Security Administration has a Web site with publications that explain social security and survivor benefits.

 THE SOCIAL SECURITY ADMINISTRATION
http://www.ssa.gov

Any pension or annuity check received after the date of death of a federal retiree, or a survivor annuitant, needs to be returned to the U.S. Treasury. If the check is direct deposited to a bank account, call the financial institution and ask them to return the check. If the check is sent by mail, you need to return it to the return mail address on the Department of Treasury envelop in which the check was mailed. Include a letter explaining the reason for the return of the check and stating the decedent's date of death.

$$$ APPLY FOR BENEFITS $$$

A survivor annuity may be available to a surviving spouse, and/or minor or disabled child. In some cases, a former spouse may be eligible for benefits. Even though you notify the government of the death, they will not automatically give you benefits to which you may be entitled. You need to apply for those benefits by notifying the Office of Personnel Management ("OPM") of the death and requesting that they send you an application for survivor benefits. You can call them at (888) 767-6738 or you can write to:

U. S. OFFICE OF PERSONNEL MANAGEMENT
RETIREMENT OPERATIONS CENTER
Post Office Box 45
Boyers, PA 16017-4500

You will find brochures and information about Survivor's Benefits at the OPM Web site.

 U.S. OFFICE OF PERSONNEL MANAGEMENT
http://www.opm.gov

> **Special Situation**

DECEDENT WITH AN ANNUITY OR A COMPANY PENSION

In most cases, pension and annuity checks are payment for the prior month. If the decedent received his pension or annuity check before his death, then no monies need be returned. Pension checks and/or annuity checks received after the date of death may need to be returned to the company. You need to notify the company of the death to determine the status of the last check sent to the decedent.

Before notifying the company, locate the policy or pension statement that is the basis of the income. That document should tell whether there is a beneficiary of the pension or annuity funds now that the pensioner or annuitant is dead. If you cannot locate the document, use the return address on the check envelope and ask the company to send you a copy of the plan. Also request that they forward to you any claim form that may be required in order for the survivor or beneficiary to receive benefits under that pension plan or policy.

If the pension/annuity check is direct-deposited to the decedent's account, then ask the bank to assist you in locating the company and notifying the company of the death.

Anyone who is a beneficiary of an Individual Retirement Account ("IRA") or QRP needs to keep in mind that income taxes may not have been paid on monies placed in an IRA or QRP account. In such case, significant taxes may be due when the money is withdrawn. You need to learn what options are available to you as a beneficiary of the plan and the tax consequences of each option. You will need to ask an accountant how much will be due in taxes for each option. Once you know all the facts, you will be able to make the best choice for your circumstance.

There are special options available if the spouse is the beneficiary of the decedent's IRA account. The spouse has the right to withdraw the money from the account or roll it over into the spouse's own retirement account. Although the employer can explain options that are available, the spouse still needs to understand the tax consequence of choosing any given option. It is important to consult with an accountant to determine the best way to go.

If the decedent had a QRP, the plan may permit the spouse to roll the balance of the account into a new IRA. The spouse needs to contact the decedent's employer for an explanation of the plan and all the options that are available at this time.

NOTIFYING IRS

THE FINAL INCOME TAX RETURN

The decedent's final income tax return (IRS form 1040) needs to be filed by April 15th of the year following the year in which he died. The Massachusetts state income tax is filed at the same time.

If the decedent was married, the surviving spouse can file a final joint return. If there is no surviving spouse, then it is the Personal Representative's job to file the final returns. If no Probate procedure is necessary, whoever inherits the decedent's property needs to file the final income tax returns. If you have a joint bank account with the decedent, you may want to keep the account open until you determine whether the decedent is entitled to an income tax refund. See Chapter 6 for an explanation of how to obtain an income tax refund.

THE GOOD NEWS

Monies inherited from the decedent are generally not counted as income to you, so you do not pay federal income tax on those monies. If the monies you inherit later earn interest or income for you, then of course you will report that income as you do any other type of income.

┌─────────┐
│ SPOUSE │ ───── SELLING THE HOMESTEAD
└─────────┘

In the tough "ole days" the IRS used to allow capital gains tax exclusion (up to $125,000) on the sale of one's *homestead* (the principal residence). A person had to be 55 or older to take advantage of the exclusion, and it was a once-in-a-lifetime tax break. If a married couple sold their home and took the exclusion it was "used up" and no longer available to either partner.

In these, the good times, the IRS allows you to sell your home and up to $250,000 ($500,000 for a married couple) of the home-sale profit is tax free. There is no limit on the number of times you can use the exclusion, provided you own and live in the home at least two of the last five years prior to the sale (26 U.S.C. 121).

If, under the old law, the decedent and his spouse used their "once in a lifetime" homestead tax exclusion, with this new law, the surviving spouse can sell the home and once again take advantage of a tax break.

WIDOW(ER)'S HOMESTEAD TAX REDUCTION

If the decedent's spouse owns a Massachusetts residence or a residence is occupied by the decedent's minor child then the spouse or minor child may be eligible for a reduction in taxes. The amount of reductions varies depending the value of the property, its location; whether the decedent died while in the armed forced or while performing a public service such as fireman or policeman. The surviving spouse or guardian of the decedent's minor child needs to notify the local Tax Board of the death and then request information whether he/she is eligible for a reduction in property taxes (MGL 59.5 Clauses 17, 22, 41, 42).

| Special Situation | > BENEFICIARY OF REAL PROPERTY |

In Massachusetts, a person can get up to $300,000 homestead creditor protection by filing a **Declaration of Homestead** with the Registry of Deeds. Once filed the property becomes an ***Estate of Homestead*** and the property is protected from forced sale, with the exception of mortgages placed on the property (MGL 188:1). See page 88 for other exceptions.

If you inherit property in Massachusetts and you intend to occupy the property as your primary residence, you can obtain this creditor protection by filing your own Declaration of Homestead with the Registry of Deeds in the county where the property is located. You can get the Declaration form and other information by searching the word "Homestead" at the Massachusetts Web site: http://www.state.ma.us.

Homestead creditor protection extends to the surviving spouse and minor child, giving them the right to continue to live in your property should you die. Before establishing an Estate of Homestead, you may want to read Page 107:
AN INVISIBLE LIFE ESTATE.

If you inherited the decedent's Homestead property as a surviving spouse or a surviving joint owner of the property, then you should check with the Registry of Deeds to determine whether you need to file your own Declaration of Homestead at this time.

Massachusetts also has certain homestead tax breaks for disabled residents (See Chapter 4). You may want to check with the local Tax Board if you think you may be eligible.

AN ESTATE TAX FOR THE WEALTHY

Both the federal and state government have the right to impose an *Estate Tax* on property transferred to a beneficiary as a result of the death. All the property owned as of the date of death becomes the decedent's *Taxable Estate.* This includes *real property* (residential lots, condominiums etc.) and *personal property* (life insurance policies, cars, business interests, securities, IRA accounts, etc.). It includes property held in the decedent's name alone, as well as property that he held jointly or in Trust. It also includes gifts given by the decedent during his lifetime that exceeded $10,000 per person, per year. In the year 2002, the *Annual Gift Tax Exclusion* was adjusted for inflation to $11,000 (IRC 2503(b)).

For most of us, this is not a concern because no federal Estate Tax need be paid unless the decedent's Taxable Estate exceeds the federal *Estate Tax Exclusion* amount. That value is currently one and a half million dollars and is scheduled to go even higher:

YEAR	ESTATE TAX EXCLUSION AMOUNT
2004-2005	$1,500,000
2006-2008	$2,000,000
2009	$3,500,000

In 2010 the federal Estate Tax is scheduled to be phased out altogether; however in 2011, the Estate Tax will be reinstated with an Exclusion Amount of $1,000,000, unless lawmakers change the law again.

There is an unlimited marital tax deduction for property transferred to the surviving spouse; so in most cases, no Estate tax need be paid if the decedent was married. Regardless of whether taxes are due, federal and state Estate Tax returns must be filed whenever the decedent's Estate exceeds the federal Estate Tax Exclusion Amount in effect as of his date of death (MGL 65C:2A).

THE UN-UNIFIED GIFT TAX

Up until the year 2002, if you gave someone more than $10,000 in any given year you had to report that gift to the IRS. As explained, the Annual Gift Tax Exclusion is now adjusted for the cost of living and is currently $11,000. The IRS keeps a running count of amounts that you give over the Annual Gift Tax Exclusion each year. Although you are required to report the gift, no tax need be paid unless that running total is more than the federal Estate Tax Exclusion amount. If your running total does not exceed that amount during your lifetime, once you die, the cumulative value of gifts reported to the IRS will be added to your Taxable Estate.

Until the tax law was changed, the Gift and Estate tax were unified. No Gift Tax needed to be paid unless the total value of the taxable gifts exceeded the federal Estate Tax Exclusion amount. In 2004 that changed. The Estate Tax Exclusion amount went up to $1,500,000, but the amount for the Gift Tax Exclusion remained at $1,000,000, so they now are no longer unified.

To summarize:
If you make a gift to anyone that is greater than the Annual Gift Tax Exclusion for that year, you must report the gift to the IRS. The IRS will keep count of values that you gave in excess of the Annual Gift Tax Exclusion. In 2004, and thereafter, if that sum exceeds $1,000,000, you will pay a Gift Tax on any amount that you give that is over the Annual Gift Tax Exclusion.

The Estate Tax is scheduled to be repealed in 2010, but not the Gift Tax.

Massachusetts does not have a Gift Tax at this time.

The current federal Estate tax is scheduled to be phased out in the year 2010, but a new Capital Gains Tax is scheduled for 2010 that may prove even more costly than the Estate Tax. The new Capital Gains Tax is related to the way inherited property is evaluated by the federal government. Real and personal property is inherited at a "step up" in basis, meaning that if the decedent's property has increased in value from the time he acquired it, the beneficiary will inherit the property at its fair market value as of the decedent's date of death. For example, if the decedent bought stock for $20,000 and it is worth $50,000 as of his date of death, the beneficiary will take a step-up in basis of $30,000; i.e. the beneficiary inherits the stock at the current $50,000 value. If the beneficiary sells the stock for $50,000, he pays no Capital Gains Tax. If the beneficiary holds onto the stock and later sells it for $60,000, the beneficiary will pay a Capital Gains Tax only on the $10,000 increase in value since the decedent's death.

Up to 2009, there is no limit to the amount a beneficiary can take as a step-up in basis. But in 2010 caps are set in place. The decedent's Estate will be allowed a 1.3 million dollar step-up in basis, plus another 3 million for property passing to the surviving spouse. The new law could result in significant Capital Gains Taxes that the beneficiary must pay. For example, suppose in 2010 you inherit a business from your father that he purchased for $100,000 and it is now worth 2 million dollars. There is a capital gain of 1.9 million dollars, but you are allowed a step-up in basis of only 1.3 million. If you sell it for 2 million dollars $600,000 of your inheritance will be subject to a Capital Gains Tax.

DECEDENT WITH A TRUST

If the decedent was the Grantor (or Settlor) of a Trust, that he established during his lifetime, then he was probably managing the Trust, as Trustee. The Trust document should name someone as **Successor Trustee** now that the Grantor is deceased. The Trust document may instruct the Successor Trustee to make certain gifts once the Grantor dies, or perhaps hold money in trust for a beneficiary of the Trust.

IF YOU ARE SUCCESSOR TRUSTEE

If you are the Successor Trustee, then in addition to following the terms of the Trust, you are required to obey the laws of the state of Massachusetts relating to the administration of a Trust. For example, you may not transfer a gift of more than $10,000 to someone under 18, or even to his parent for the benefit of the minor, without permission from the Probate Court (MGL 201A:6). It is prudent to consult with an attorney experienced in Trust and Estate matters to explain how to properly administer the Trust and to ensure that you do so without any liability to yourself.

IF YOU ARE A BENEFICIARY

If you are a beneficiary of the Trust, then you need to obtain a copy of the Trust and see how the Trust is to be administered now that the Grantor or Settlor is deceased. Most Trust documents are written in "legalese," so you may want to employ your own attorney to review the Trust, and explain what rights you have under that Trust.

NOTIFYING THE BUSINESS COMMUNITY

People and companies who were doing business with the decedent need to be notified of his death. This includes utility companies, credit card companies, banks, brokerage firms and any company that insured the decedent.

NOTIFY CREDIT CARD COMPANIES

You need to notify the decedent's credit card companies of the death. If you can find the contract with the credit card company check to see whether the decedent had credit card insurance. If the decedent had credit card insurance, then the balance of the account is now paid in full. If you cannot find the contract contact the company and get a copy of the contract along with a statement of the balance due as of the date of death.

DESTROY DECEDENT'S CREDIT CARDS

You need to destroy all of the decedent's credit cards. If you hold a credit card jointly with the decedent, then it is important to waste no time in closing that account and opening another in your name only.

That's something Barbara knows from hard experience. She and Hank lived together but never married. When Hank came down with hepatitis, she cared for him at home. Hank came from a well to do family. They supported the couple during Hank's long illness. Hank put Barbara on all of his credit card accounts so that she could purchase things when he became too ill to go shopping with her.

After the funeral, Barbara had a gathering of friends and family at their apartment. Barbara was so preoccupied with her loss that she never noticed that Hank's credit cards were missing until the bills started coming in.

Barbara did not know who ran up the bills on Hank's credit cards during the month following his death. It was obvious that Hank's signature had been forged — but who forged it? One credit card company suspected that it might have been Barbara herself to get out of paying the bill by saying that the card was stolen.

Because the cards were held jointly, the company held Barbara liable to either pay the charges or prove that she did not make the purchases. She was able to clear her credit record but it took several months and she had to employ an attorney to do so.

NOTIFY INSURANCE COMPANIES

If the decedent had life insurance, you need to locate the policy and notify the company of his death. Call each life insurance company and ask what they require in order to forward the insurance proceeds to the beneficiary. Most companies will ask you to send them the original policy and a certified copy of the death certificate. Send the original policy by certified mail or any of the overnight services that require a signed receipt for the package. Make a copy of the original policy for your records before mailing the original policy to the company.

BANK ACCOUNT LIFE INSURANCE

Many banks, credit unions, savings and loan associations provide life insurance at no cost to the primary owner of the account. While the amounts are generally small ($1,000 to $5,000), it is insurance that is often overlooked when settling the decedent's affairs. If you do not find a record of such policy, contact each financial institution to determine whether such insurance is provided by the company.

If you know that the decedent was insured, but you cannot locate the insurance policy, you can contact the company and request a copy of the policy. A tougher question is how to locate the policy if you can't find the policy and do not know the name of the insurance company. The American Council of Life Insurers offers suggestions that you may find helpful at the Missing Policy Inquiry page of their Web site.

 AMERICAN COUNCIL OF LIFE INSURERS
http://www.acli.com

IF YOU CANNOT LOCATE THE COMPANY

If you cannot locate the insurance company it may be doing business under another name or it may no longer be doing business in the state of Massachusetts. Insurance companies are highly regulated. Each state has a branch of government that regulates insurance companies. If you are having difficulty locating the insurance company call the Department of Insurance in the state where the policy was purchased and ask for assistance in locating the company. The number for the Massachusetts Division of Insurance is (617) 521-7777.

You can find the telephone number of the Department of Insurance of other states at the Public Information section of the Eagle Publishing Company Web site.
http://www.eaglepublishing.com

HOMEOWNER'S INSURANCE

If the decedent owned his own home, then check whether there is sufficient insurance coverage on the property. The decedent may have neglected to increase his insurance as the property appreciated in value. If you think the property may be vacant for some period of time, then consider having vandalism coverage included in the policy.

Once the property is sold, or transferred to the proper beneficiary, you can have the policy discontinued or transferred to the new owner. The decedent's Estate should receive a rebate for the unused portion of the premium.

NOTIFYING THE HOMEOWNER'S ASSOCIATION

If the decedent owned a condominium or a residence regulated by a homeowner's association, then the association needs to be notified of the death. Once the property is transferred to the proper beneficiary, he will need to contact the association and arrange to have notices of dues or assessments forwarded to him.

MORTGAGE INSURANCE

If the decedent had a mortgage on any parcel of real estate that he owned, he might have arranged with his lender for an insurance policy that pays off the mortgage balance in the event of his death. Look at the closing statement to see if there was a charge for mortgage insurance. Also, check with the lender to determine if such a policy was purchased.

If there is no insurance policy and decedent was the sole owner of the property, the beneficiary of that property needs to make arrangements with the lender to continue payment of the mortgage, or to refinance the loan.

MOTOR VEHICLE INSURANCE

Locate the insurance policy for all motor vehicles owed by the decedent (car, truck, snowmobile, boat, airplane) and notify the insurance company of the death. Determine how long insurance coverage continues after the death. Ask the insurance agent to explain what things are covered under the policy. Is the motor vehicle covered for all types of casualty (theft, accident, vandalism, etc.) or is coverage limited in some way?

If you can continue coverage, then determine when the next insurance payment is due. Hopefully, the car will be sold or transferred to a beneficiary before that date, but if not, you need to arrange for sufficient insurance coverage during the Probate procedure.

 *Special Situation* ACCIDENTAL DEATH

If the decedent died as a result of an accident, then check for all possible sources of accident insurance coverage including his homeowner's policy. Some credit card companies provide free accident insurance as part of their contract with their card holders. If the decedent died in an automobile accident, then check to see whether he was covered by any type of travel insurance, such as rental car insurance. If he belonged to an automobile club, such as AAA, then check whether he had insurance as part of his club membership.

WORK RELATED INSURANCE

If the decedent was employed then his employer may provide survivor benefits from a company or a group life insurance plan and/or a retirement plan. If the decedent belonged to a union, then check with the union to determine whether members of the union receive any death benefits.

BUSINESS OWNED BY DECEDENT

If the decedent owned his own company, he may have purchased "key man" insurance. Key man insurance is a policy designed to protect the company should a valuable employee become disabled or die. Benefits are paid to the company to compensate the company for the loss of someone who is essential to the continuation of the business. Ultimately the policy benefits those who inherit the business.

If the decedent owned shares in a company or was a partner in a company, there may be a shareholder's or partnership agreement requiring the company to purchase the decedent's share of the business.

If the decedent had an ownership interest in an ongoing business (sole proprietor, shareholder or partner), the Personal Representative's attorney needs to investigate to see if there was a key man insurance policy and/or such purchase agreement.

ORGANIZATIONAL INSURANCE

The decedent may have belonged to a professional, fraternal or social organization such as the local Chamber of Commerce, a Veteran's organization, the Kiwanis, AARP, the Rotary Club, etc. If he belonged to such an organization check to see whether the organization provided any type of insurance coverage.

If the decedent was a director or an officer (president, treasurer, clerk or resident agent) of a Massachusetts corporation, then within 30 days of the death the Corporations Division of the Office of the Secretary of the Commonwealth needs to be notified of the death and of the identity of the new officer or director. If the corporation fails (or refuses) to file a Certificate of Change within that time, then the Personal Representative can do so, provided he mails a copy of the Certificate to the principal office of the Corporation (MGL 156B:53).

You can get the Certificate of Change form by calling the Corporations Division at (617) 727-9640 or by visiting their Web site:

 MASSACHUSETTS CORPORATION DIVISION
http://www.state.ma.us/sec/cor

STATUS REPORT

If you were not actively involved in running the business, then you might want to see a status report of the company. The report will show whether filing fees are current and will identify the officers and directors of the company. You can obtain a status report by calling the above number or by writing to:

Secretary of the Commonwealth
Corporation Division
1 Ashburton Place, 17th floor
Boston, MA 02108

HEALTH INSURANCE

If the decedent had health insurance, then the insurance carrier probably knows of the death, but it is a good idea to contact them to determine what coverage the decedent had under that insurance plan. If you cannot find the original policy, have the insurance company send you a copy of the policy so you can determine whether medical treatment rendered to the decedent before his death was covered by that policy.

 Special Situation **DECEDENT ON MEDICARE**

If the decedent was covered by Medicare, you do not need to notify anyone, but you do need to know what things were covered by Medicare so that you can determine what medical bills are (or are not) covered by Medicare. The government publication MEDICARE AND YOU (Publication No. CMS-10050) explains what things are covered under Medicare and the different kinds of plans that are currently available. You can get the publication by writing to:

U.S. Dept. of Health and Human Services
Centers for Medicare and Medicaid Services
7500 Security Boulevard
Baltimore, MD 21244-1850

You can download the publication from the Internet.

 MEDICARE WEB SITE
http://www.medicare.gov

The publication is available on Audiotape, in Braille, in large print and in Spanish. To receive a copy you can call (800) 633-4227. TTY users call (877) 486-2048.

HEALTH INSURANCE COVERAGE FOR THE SPOUSE

SPOUSE

If the spouse is covered under Medicare, then the death does not affect the spouse's coverage. But if the spouse was covered under the decedent's private health insurance policy then he/she needs to arrange for new coverage. If the decedent was employed by a federally regulated company (a company with at least twenty employees), then under the Consolidated Omnibus Budget Reconciliation Act ("COBRA") the employer must make the company health plan available to the surviving spouse and any dependent child of the decedent for at least 36 months. The employer must notify the spouse and/or dependent child of their right to continue insurance coverage. They have 60 days from the date of death or 60 days after notice is sent by the employer (whichever is later) to notify the employer whether they wish to continue under the plan.

The only problem with continued coverage may be the cost. Before the death, the employer may have been paying some percentage of the premium. The employer has no such duty after the death unless there was some employment agreement stating otherwise. Under COBRA, the employer may charge the spouse for the full cost of the plan plus a 2% administrative fee. If you have a question about your coverage under COBRA, you can call the U.S. Department of Labor ("DOL") at (800) 998-7542 and ask for the number of your local DOL office. You can also ask that they send you their publication HEALTH BENEFITS UNDER COBRA; or you can visit their Web site for more information.

U. S. DEPARTMENT OF LABOR
http://www.dol.gov/dol/pwba

MASSACHUSETTS NONGROUP HEALTH INSURANCE

Chapter 176M of the Massachusetts General Laws makes provision for health care insurance coverage for those Massachusetts residents who are not eligible for employer-based health insurance coverage. If surviving spouse is unable to continue coverage under the decedent's plan, then the spouse may be eligible to obtain Nongroup Health Insurance coverage from an insurance company under the state plan. For information about insurance plans that may provide coverage call the Massachusetts Division of Insurance at (617) 521-7777.

Massachusetts also has a program that helps to pay health insurance premiums for Massachusetts residents who are disabled or unemployed. You can get information about the program by calling (800) 841-2900.

The Massachusetts Division of Insurance has a Web site with information about these programs:

 MASSACHUSETTS DIVISION OF INSURANCE
http://www.state.ma.us/doi/

Whether or not the decedent's health insurance coverage falls under COBRA, it is important that the surviving spouse contact the employer, and the insurer, to learn of his/her options relating to continued coverage, or converting to a new health insurance policy, as soon as is practical after the death.

✍ CHANGE BENEFICIARY ✍

If the decedent was someone you named as beneficiary of your insurance policy, Will or trust, brokerage account or pension plan, then you may need to name another beneficiary in his place:

INSURANCE POLICY ✍

If you named the decedent as the primary beneficiary of your life insurance policy, check to see whether you named a contingent (alternate) beneficiary in the event that the decedent did not survive you. If not, you need to contact the insurance company and name a new beneficiary. If you did name a contingent beneficiary, that person is now your primary beneficiary and you need to consider whether you wish to name a new contingent beneficiary at this time.

HEALTH INSURANCE POLICY ✍

If the decedent was covered under your health insurance policy, your employer and the health insurer need to be notified of the death because this may affect the cost of the plan to you and/or your employer.

WILL OR TRUST ✍

Most Wills provide for a contingent beneficiary in the event that the person named as beneficiary dies first. If you named the decedent as your beneficiary, check to see whether you named an alternate beneficiary. If not, you need to have your attorney revise your Will and name a new beneficiary.

Similarly, if you are the Grantor or Settlor of a Trust and the decedent was one of the beneficiaries of your Trust, check the Trust document to see if you named an alternate beneficiary. If not, contact your attorney to prepare an amendment to the Trust, naming a new beneficiary.

BANK AND SECURITIES ACCOUNTS ✍

If the decedent was a beneficiary or joint owner of your bank or securities account, it is important to contact the financial institution and tell them about the death. You may wish to arrange for a new beneficiary or joint owner at this time.

PENSION PLANS ✍

If the decedent was a beneficiary under your pension plan, you need to notify them of his death and name a new beneficiary. Many pension plans require that you notify them within a set period of time (usually 30 days) so it is important to notify them as soon as you are able. If the decedent was a beneficiary of your Individual Retirement Account ("IRA") or of your Qualified Retirement Plan ("QRP") and you did not provide for an alternate beneficiary, you need to name another beneficiary at this time.

Before you choose an alternate beneficiary, it is important that you understand all of the options available to you. Not an easy task. There are many complex government regulations relating to IRA and QRP accounts. Even if you believe you understood your options when you set up your account, the federal government often changes those options.

Your choice of beneficiary might impact the amount of money you can withdraw each month, so it is important to consult with your accountant or tax attorney or financial planner, before you make your election.

NOTIFY ADVERTISERS

Probably the last in the world to learn of the decedent's death is the direct mail advertiser. Advertisers are nothing if not tenacious. It is not uncommon for advertisements to be mailed to the decedent for more than ten years after the death. It is not because the advertiser is trying to sell something to the decedent, but rather the people who prepare (and sell) mailing lists do not know that the person is dead.

Those who sell mailing lists may not be motivated to update the list because of the cost of doing the necessary research; and perhaps because the price of the mailing list is often based on the number of people on the list. Even those who compose their own list may decide it is less costly to mail to everyone, than take the time (and money) to update the list.

If it gives you pleasure to think of advertisers spending substantial sums for nothing, then that is what you should do (nothing). But for those of you who wince each time you see another piece of mail addressed to the decedent, you can write to the Direct Marketing Association and ask that the decedent's name be deleted from all mailing lists:

Mail Preference Service
Direct Marketing Association
P.O. Box 9008
Farmingdale, NY 11735

You will need to give them the decedent's complete address, including zip code and name variations that the decedent may have used; for example:

Mr. Theodore James Jones
Ted Jones   Ted J. Jones
T. J. Jones   T. James Jones, etc.

NOTIFYING CREDITORS

It is the job of the person appointed as Personal Representative to notify the decedent's creditors of the death so that the creditor is given an opportunity to come forward and present a *claim* (a written demand for payment) for monies owed. The attorney for the Personal Representative usually takes care of the notice procedure, but see Chapter 4 for an explanation what is involved.

If no Probate procedure is necessary, then the next of kin can notify the creditors of the death, but before doing so, read Chapter 4: WHAT BILLS NEED TO BE PAID? That chapter explains what bills need to be paid and who is responsible to pay them.

Before any bill can be paid you need to know whether the decedent left any assets that could be used to pay those debts. The next chapter explains how to identify, and then locate all of the property owned by the decedent.

Locating the Assets 3

It is important to locate the financial records of the decedent and then carefully examine those records. Even the partner of a long-term marriage should conduct a thorough search because the surviving spouse may be unaware of all that was owned (or owed) by the decedent.

It is not unusual for a surviving spouse to be surprised when learning of the decedent's business transactions, especially in those cases where the decedent had control of family finances. One such example is that of Sam and Helen. They married just as soon as Sam was discharged from the army after World War II. During their marriage, Sam handled all of the finances, giving Helen just enough money to run the household.

Every now and again Helen would think of getting a job. She longed to have her own source of income and some economic independence. Each time she brought up the subject Sam would loudly object. He had no patience for this new "woman's lib" thing. Sam said he got married to have a real wife — one who would cook his meals and keep house for him.

Helen was not the arguing type. She rationalized, saying that Sam had a delicate stomach and dust allergies. He needed her to prepare his special meals and keep an immaculate house for him. Besides, Sam had a good job with a major cruise line and he needed her to accompany him on his frequent business trips.

Once Sam retired, he was even more cautious in his spending habits. Helen seldom complained. She assumed the reason for his "thrift" was that they had little money and had to live on his pension.

They were married 52 years when Sam died at the age of 83. Helen was 81 at the time of his death. She was one very happy, very angry and very aged widow when she discovered that Sam left her with assets worth well over a million dollars!

LOCATING RECORDS

As you go through the papers of the decedent you may come across documents that indicate property ownership, such as bank registers, stock or bond certificates, insurance policies, brokerage account statements, etc. Place all evidence of ownership in a single place. You will need to contact the different companies in order to transfer title to the proper beneficiary. Chapter 5 explains how to identify the proper beneficiary of the decedent's property. Chapter 6 explains how to transfer the property to that beneficiary.

You may also need to produce evidence of the decedent's relationship to the beneficiary, such as a marriage certificate, birth certificate, or naturalization papers, a Final Judgement of Divorce, military personnel records, etc. If you cannot locate his marriage certificate or birth certificate, you can get a certified copy of those records from the Vital Records office in the state where the event took place. See page 24 Massachusetts' Vital Records. You can find the location and telephone number for other states by calling information or from the Internet by using your favorite search engine to locate Vital Records.

You can obtain a copy of the military records of a deceased veteran by writing to:

The National Personnel Records Center
Military Personnel Records
9700 Page Avenue
St. Louis, MO   63132-5100

They will send you form SF 180 to complete. You can get the form from the Internet at http://www.cem.va.gov or from the National Archives and Records Administration Fax-On-Demand system. Dial (301) 713-6905 and request document number 2255.

COLLECT AND IDENTIFY KEYS

The decedent may have kept his records in a safe deposit box, so you may find that your first job is to locate the keys to the box. As you go through the personal effects of the decedent, collect and identify all the keys that you find. If you come across an unidentified key, it could be a key to a post office box (private or federal) or a safe deposit box located in a bank or in a private vault company. You need to determine whether that key opens a box that contains property belonging to the decedent or whether the key is to a box no longer in use. Some ways to investigate are as follows:

☑ CHECK BUSINESS RECORDS

If the decedent kept receipts, look through those items to see if he paid for the rental of a post office or safe deposit box. Also, look at his check register to see if he wrote a check to the Postmaster or to any safe deposit or vault company. Look at his bank statements to see if there is any bank charge for a safe deposit box. Some banks bill separately for a safe deposit box so check with all of the banks in which the decedent had an account to determine whether he had a safe deposit box with that bank.

☑ CHECK THE KEY TYPE

If you cannot identify the key, then take it to each local locksmith and ask whether anyone can identify the type of facility that uses such keys. If that doesn't work, then go to each bank, post office and private safe deposit box company where the decedent shopped, worked or frequented and ask whether they use the type of key that you found.

☑ CHECK THE MAIL

Check the mail over the next several months to see if the decedent receives a statement requesting payment for the next year's rental of a post office or safe deposit box.

You may find evidence of a brokerage account, bank account, or safe deposit box by examining correspondence addressed to the decedent. If the decedent was living alone, have the mail forwarded to the person he named as Personal Representative or Executor of his Will. If the decedent did not leave a Will, the mail should be forwarded to his next of kin. Call the Postmaster and ask him to send you the necessary forms to make the change. Request that the mail be forwarded for the longest period allowed by law (currently one year).

The decedent may have been renting a post office box at his local post office branch or perhaps at the branch closest to where he did his banking. Ask the Postmaster to help you determine whether the decedent was renting a post office box. If so, then you need to locate the key to the box so that you can collect the decedent's mail.

 LOST POST OFFICE BOX KEY

If the decedent had a post office box and you cannot locate the key, then contact the local postmaster and ask him/her what documentation is needed for you to gain possession of the mail in that box. As before, you will ask the Postmaster to have all future mail addressed to that box, forwarded to the Personal Representative, or if no Probate is necessary, then to the decedent's next of kin.

WHAT TO DO WITH CHECKS

You may receive checks in the mail made out to the decedent. Social security checks, pension checks and annuity checks issued after the date of death may need to be returned to the sender. (See pages 28 and 30 of this book.) Other checks need to be deposited. If a Probate procedure is necessary, then the Personal Representative will open a Probate Estate account and will deposit the decedent's checks to that account.

If no Probate procedure is necessary, then checks can be deposited to any account held in the name of the decedent. The decedent is not here to endorse the check, but you can deposit it to his account by writing his bank account number on the back of the check and printing beneath it **FOR DEPOSIT ONLY**. The bank will accept such an endorsement and deposit the check into the decedent's account. If the check is significant in value or the decedent had different accounts that are accessible to different people, then there needs to be cooperation and a sense of fair play. If not, the dollar gain may not nearly offset the emotional turmoil.

That was the case with Gail. Her father made her a joint owner of his checking account to assist in paying his bills. He had macular degeneration and it was increasingly difficult for him to see. The father also had a savings account that was in his name only.

Gail's brother Ken had a good paying job in southern California. Even though he lived at a distance, Ken, his wife and two children always spent the spring break with his father. Gail's good cooking added to the festivities.

The father enjoyed taking a reprieve from the rigors of the Massachusetts winter by spending a few weeks with Ken each year. One December he purchased a round trip ticket to California. It cost several hundred dollars. Before the departure date, the father had a heart attack and died.

Gail called the airline to cancel the ticket. They refunded the money in a check made out to her father. She deposited the check to the joint account, and then closed it out.

As part of the Probate procedure, the money in the father's savings account was divided equally between Ken and his sister. Ken wondered what happened to the money from the airline tickets.

Gail explained "Dad paid for the tickets from the joint account, so I deposited the money back to that account. "

"Aren't you going to give me half?"

"Dad meant for me to have whatever was in that joint account. If he wanted you to have half of the money, he would have made you joint owner as well."

Ken didn't see it that way "That refund was part of Dad's Estate. It should have been deposited to his savings account to be divided equally between us. Are you going to force me to argue this in Court?"

Gail finally agreed to split the money with Ken, but the damage was done.

Gail complains that holidays are lonely since Dad died.

LOCATING FINANCIAL RECORDS

To locate the decedent's assets you need to find evidence of what he owned and where those assets are located. His financial records should lead you to the location of all of his assets, so your first job is to locate those records. The best place to start the search is in the decedent's home. Many people keep their financial records in a single place but it is important to check the entire house to be sure you did not miss something.

CHECK THE COMPUTER

Don't overlook that computer sitting silently in the corner. It may hold the decedent's check register and all of the decedent's financial records. The computer may be programmed to protect information. If you cannot access the decedent's records, you may need to employ a computer technician or computer consultant who will be able to print out all of the information on the hard drive of the computer. You can find such a technician or consultant by looking in the telephone book under
COMPUTER SUPPORT SERVICES   or
COMPUTER SYSTEM DESIGNS & CONSULTANTS.

LOCATE TITLE TO MOTOR VEHICLE

In Massachusetts, if monies are owed on a motor vehicle (car, boat, snowmobile), the lender takes possession of the certificate of title until the loan is paid. If you cannot find the original certificate of title, it is either lost or monies are owed on the car and the lienholder has it. To get information about the title to the car, you can go to the local Registry of Motor Vehicles. You can find the location of the nearest Registry by visiting their Web site.

 MASSACHUSETTS REGISTRY OF MOTOR VEHICLES
http:www.state.ma.us/rev/

If you find there is a lien on the motor vehicle, contact the lienholder and get a copy of the contract that is the basis of the loan. If the original title to the car is lost, you can apply for a duplicate Certificate of Title by writing to:

REGISTRY OF MOTOR VEHICLES, TITLE DIVISION
P.O. Box 199136
Boston, MA 02119-9136

They currently charge $25 for a duplicate title. You may first want to call them at (617) 351-4500 to find out what information and documentation they may require. To get a duplicate title to the a motorboat or snowmobile call (617) 727-3900.

THE LEASED CAR

You may find that the car is leased and not owned by the decedent. If so, contact the lessor and get a copy of the lease agreement. Check to see whether the decedent had life insurance as part of the agreement. If he did, the lease may now be paid in full and the beneficiary of the car should be able to use the car for the remainder of the leasing period, or take title to the car, whichever option is available under the lease agreement.

THE MOBILE HOME

In Massachusetts, mobile homes are titled and registered in the same manner as any other motor vehicle. If the decedent owned a parcel of land and his mobile home was permanently attached to that land, then turn to Chapter 6 for information about transferring the land and the mobile home to the proper beneficiary. If the decedent owned a mobile home that is kept in a leased space, you need to locate the lease to the mobile home lot. If you cannot locate the lease, contact the landlord for a copy, and proceed in the same manner as for a residential lease (see page 67).

LOCATE TITLE TO MOTORBOAT

All motorboats used primarily in Massachusetts, that are at least 14' in length must have a certificate of title. If the decedent owned a boat, you should be able to locate the title and registration to the boat. The Registration and Titling Section of the Massachusetts Department of Fisheries, Wildlife and Environmental Law Enforcement is responsible for titling and registering motorboats, all-terrain-vehicles and snowmobiles. If you cannot locate the title and registration, you can their Boston office at (517) 626-1610 for information about obtaining a duplicate title (MGL 90B:36).

LOCATE TITLE TO AIRCRAFT

If the decedent owned an aircraft, then you should find a certificate of title to the aircraft. The Civil Aviation Registry of the Federal Aviation Administration ("FAA") contains all of the ownership and security documents that have been filed with the FAA. If you cannot locate title to the aircraft you can contact the Civil Aviation Registry. They do not perform title searches, however they can give you a list of title search companies. If you wish to perform the title search yourself you can call the Aircraft Registration Branch at (405) 954-3116 for more information or you can visit the FAA Web site.

 THE FEDERAL AVIATION ADMINISTRATION
http://www2.faa.gov

Massachusetts law requires that the federal certificate be registered with the MASSACHUSETTS AERONAUTICS COMMISSION so you should also find a Massachusetts Registration Certificate (MGL 90:49). If you cannot locate the Certificate you can call the Commission and ask for a duplicate. Their number is (617) 973-8881.

COLLECT DEEDS

Collect deeds to all of the property owned by the decedent. In addition to the deed, look for other documents associated with the title to the land, such as a mortgage. You may come across a title insurance policy. The new owner can turn in that policy and might be able to receive a discount toward the purchase of the new title insurance; so it is important to keep the policy together with the deed.

Instead of a title insurance policy you may find an *Abstract of Title*. An Abstract of Title is a summary of the documents or facts appearing on the public record which affect title to the property. The Abstract will need to be updated once the property is transferred. We will discuss the transfer of property in Chapter 6.

Many people keep deeds in a safe deposit box. If you cannot find the deed in the decedent's home, then you need to determine whether he had a safe deposit box; and if so, you will need to examine the contents of the box. Access to the safe deposit box is discussed at the end of this chapter.

THE LOST DEED

If you know that the decedent owned real property (lot, residence, condominium) but you cannot find the deed, contact the Registry of Deeds in the county where the property is located and ask for a copy of the deed. The Register will need to know the decedent's name and the property address. If the Register cannot locate the document, you may need to employ someone to do a title search. The Register may be able to refer a title examiner to you.

You need to locate the deed and any related document (Abstract of Title, Title Insurance policy, recorded Condominium Approval, etc.) to out of state property owned by the decedent.

THE LOST OUT OF STATE DEED

If you know the decedent owned out of state real property, you can use the same procedure just described, namely, you can check with the recording department in the county where the property is located. In some states the Clerk of the Circuit Court is in charge of the recording department. In other states it may be the County Recorder. The Clerk in the recording department should be able to give you a copy of the last recorded deed for a nominal copying fee.

If you do not know where the property is located, you will need to wait for the next tax bill. In many states the tax bill contains the legal description of the property, or its tax identification number.

Many states index the property by the name of the owner, so if you know the county where the property is located, you should be able to find the deed by giving the decedent's name to the Clerk.

| Special Situation | THE DECEDENT'S RESIDENTIAL LEASE |

THE DECEDENT'S RESIDENTIAL LEASE

Special Situation

If the decedent was renting his residence, he may have a written lease agreement. It is important to locate the lease because the decedent's Estate may be responsible for payments under the lease. If you cannot find the lease, ask the landlord for a copy. If her reports that there was no written lease, then verify that the decedent was on a month to month basis and work out a mutually agreeable time in which to vacate the premises. If a written lease is in effect, then determine the end of the lease period, and whether there was a security deposit. Ask whether the landlord will agree to cancel the lease on the condition that the property is left in good condition. If the landlord says that the Estate is responsible to pay the balance of the lease, then it is prudent to have an attorney review the lease to determine what rights and responsibilities remain now that the tenant is deceased.

AN ONGOING BUSINESS

☎ LAWYER

If the decedent was the sole owner of a business, or if he owned a partnership interest in a business, the Personal Representative needs to contact the company accountant to obtain the company's business records. If there is a company attorney, then the attorney may be able to assist in obtaining the records. If you are a beneficiary of the Estate, consider consulting with your own attorney to determine what rights and responsibilities you may have in the business.

COLLECT TAX RECORDS

The decedent's final state and federal income tax returns need to be filed so you should locate all of his tax records for the past three years. If you cannot locate his prior tax records, check his personal telephone book and/or his personal bank register to see if he employed someone to prepare his taxes. If you can locate his tax preparer, he should have a copy of those records.

If you are unable to locate the decedent's federal tax returns, they can be obtained from the IRS. The IRS will send copies of the decedent's tax filings to anyone who has a *fiduciary relationship* with the decedent. The IRS considers the following people to be a fiduciary:

➤ the person appointed as Personal Representative of the decedent's Estate

➤ the Successor Trustee of the decedent's Trust

➤ if the person died without a Will, whoever is legally entitled to possession of the decedent's See Chapter 5 for an explanation of the Laws of Descent.

The fiduciary can receive copies of the decedent's tax filings by notifying IRS that he/she is acting in a fiduciary capacity, and then requesting the copies.

To notify the IRS of the fiduciary capacity file Form 56: NOTICE CONCERNING FIDUCIARY RELATIONSHIP

Your accountant can file these forms for you or you can obtain the forms from the IRS by calling (800) 829-3676 or you can download them from the FORMS section of the IRS Web site.

 INTERNAL REVENUE SERVICE
http://www.irs.gov

STATE INCOME TAX RETURN

If you cannot locate the decedent's state income tax return you can obtain copies from the Massachusetts Department of Revenue. The Department Of Revenue will provide a copy of the decedent's return to the surviving spouse or anyone who has a Power of Attorney. If the copy of the return is requested by anyone else the Department may require that a Personal Representative be appointed by the Probate Court before they will forward a copy of the decedent's tax records.

For assistance in obtaining the copies you can call the Massachusetts Department of Revenue at (919) 733-4582; or you can write to:

Massachusetts Department of Revenue
P.O. Box 7010
Boston, MA 02204

or you can visit their Web site.

 MASSACHUSETTS DEPARTMENT OF REVENUE
http://www.state.ma.us/dor

UNCLAIMED INCOME TAX REFUND

The Massachusetts Department of Revenue's Web site contains a list of unclaimed income tax refunds, so you may want to check out whether there is a refund that is currently due to the decedent.

If the decedent was forgetful, he may have money in a bank or securities account or he may have abandoned property in his safe deposit box. Massachusetts law requires that if an account has been inactive for a period of time and the location of the owner of the property cannot be determined after a diligent search, then the property must be turned over to the State Treasurer. The period of time for declaring the property to be abandoned is usually three years, but it can vary:

⌛ 3 years for cashier's checks or certified check

⌛ 7 years for contents of a safe deposit box

⌛ 15 years for a traveler's check

Each year the State Treasurer publishes NOTICE OF NAMES APPEARING TO BE OWNERS OF ABANDONED PROPERTY in a newspaper in the county where the property is located. If no one comes forward, tangible property is sold at public auction and the proceeds turned over to the State Treasurer. Anyone who later makes a valid claim for the property will receive the cash, or net proceeds of the sale (MGL 200A:5B; 200A:6B; 200A:8; 200A:9).

For information about whether the decedent abandoned property in Massachusetts you can call the Department of State Treasurer. In state call (800) 647-2300; out of state call (617) 367-0400; or you can write to:

Massachusetts Dept of State Treasurer Abandoned Property
One Ashburton Place, 12th Floor
Boston, MA   02108

The Department of State Treasurer lists the names of persons who may have missing property in the state at their Web site.

 MASSCHUSETTS DEPARTMENT OF STATE TREASURER
http://www.magnet.state.ma.us/treasury

CLAIMS IN OTHER STATES
Each state has an agency or department that is responsible for handling lost, abandoned or unclaimed property located within that state. If the decedent had residences in other states, then call the UNCLAIMED or ABANDONED PROPERTY department of the state Treasury to see if the decedent has unclaimed property in that state.

EAGLE PUBLISHING COMPANY OF BOCA lists telephone numbers for the unclaimed property division for each state at the Public Information section of its Web site.
http://www.eaglepublishing.com

CLAIMS FOR DECEDENT VICTIMS OF HOLOCAUST
The New York State Banking Department has a special Claims Processing Office for Holocaust survivors or their heirs. The office processes claims for Swiss bank accounts that were dormant since the end of World War II. If the decedent was a victim of the Holocaust, you can get information about money that may be due to the decedent's Estate by calling (800) 695-3318.

CLAIMS FOR IRS TAX REFUNDS
The IRS reports that some 90,000 tax refund checks representing 67.4 million dollars that were returned to them as being not deliverable. They keep the information on file and will forward the full amount once they locate the taxpayer. You can determine whether they are holding a check for the decedent by calling the IRS at (800) 829-1040.

THE LOST PENSION

The decedent may be entitled to benefits under a pension plan of a prior employer. If the decedent worked for an employer for any significant period of time, say 5 years or more, then you need to check with the company benefit representative to determine whether any pension funds are payable. If you are unable to locate the former employer, then it could be that the company moved or merged with another company. There are several ways to track down the company, starting with the Secretary of State to learn of the company's current status (see page 46).

CONTACT THE UNION If company workers belonged to a union, you can contact the union and they may be able to help you locate the   company; or tell you what happened to the pension funds.

CONTACT SOCIAL SECURITY The Social Security Administration has the decedent's work record and the employer identification number for each of his employers. The Personal Representative should be able to get that information by calling the Social Security Administration at (800) 772-1213. Using the employer identification number you might be able to determine whether the pension fund has been taken over by another company.

RESEARCH THE INTERNET Pension Benefit Guaranty Corporation operates an on-line search tool for those employees whose pension plans were taken over by regulators because the company filed for bankruptcy, or because the company dissolved the plan. All you need do is go to the pension search prompt at their Web site.

 PENSION BENEFIT GUARANTY CORPORATION
http://www.pbgc.gov

LOCATE CONTRACTS

If the decedent belonged to a health club or gym, he may have prepaid for the year. Look for the club contract. It will give the terms of the agreement. If you cannot locate the contract then contact the company for a copy of the agreement. If the contract was prepaid, then determine whether the agreement provides for a refund for the unused portion; or perhaps an assignment of the unused portion to a heir of the decedent.

SERVICE CONTRACT
Many people purchase appliance service contracts to have their appliances serviced in the event that an appliance should need repair. If the decedent had a security system then he may have had a service contract with a company to monitor the system and contact the police in the event of a break-in. If the decedent had a service contract, then you need to locate it and determine whether it can be assigned to the new owner of the property. If the contract is assignable, the new owner can reimburse the decedent's Estate for the unused portion. If the contract cannot be assigned, then once the property is transferred, try to obtain a refund for the unused portion of the contract.

LOCATE OUT OF STATE ACCOUNTS

If the decedent had out of state bank or brokerage accounts, then you might be able to locate them if they mail out monthly or quarterly statements. Not all financial institutions do so, but all institutions are required to send out an IRS tax form 1099 each year giving the amount of interest earned on that account. Once those forms come in, you will learn the location of all of the decedent's active accounts.

FILING THE WILL

Massachusetts law requires that anyone in possession of the decedent's original Will must, within 30 days of being notified of the death, file the Will with the Probate Court in the county of the decedent's residence (see next page if he was not a resident). The law allows the Will to be delivered to the person named as Executor in the Will, instead of taking it to the courthouse. Once the Executor has possession of the Will, he must then deliver it to the Probate Court. Anyone who unreasonably fails to deliver the Will after being told to do so, can face jail time (MGL 191:13)

There is only one original Will, so it is important to hand carry the original document to the Clerk. If you are unable to make the delivery in person, you can mail the Will to the Clerk, but send it by registered mail so that you will have proof of delivery. Make a copy of the Will for your own records before delivering it to the Clerk.

Special Situation

WILL DRAFTED IN ANOTHER STATE OR COUNTRY

The state of Massachusetts respects the laws of other states and countries. A Will that the decedent signed in another state or country, that was in accordance with the laws of that state or country at the time it was signed, can be admitted for Probate in the state of Massachusetts (MGL 191:4, 191: 5).

If the Will is written in a foreign language, then it must be accompanied by a true and complete English translation before it can be admitted to Probate.

 **LAWYER** PROBATING OUT OF STATE
PROPERTY

If the decedent had his residence in Massachusetts and owned property in another state, you may need to have an initial Probate procedure in Massachusetts and an **ancillary** (secondary) Probate procedure in the other state. If the decedent had his residence in another state and owned property in Massachusetts, then it may need to be done the other way around; namely, you may need to conduct the initial Probate in the other state and the ancillary Probate procedure in Massachusetts (MGL 215:3).

If you are going to be Personal Representative, and the decedent owned property in another state or was a resident of another state, before depositing the Will with the Court you should consult with an experienced Probate attorney in each state to determine where the initial Probate should be conducted. Convenience is important, but there are other things to consider:
COST OF PROBATE Ask each attorney whether the location of the initial Probate procedure will have an effect on the total cost of Probate.

WHO INHERITS THE INTESTATE ESTATE Intestate laws vary significantly state to state. If the decedent died without a Will, it is important to determine whether the location of the initial Probate procedure will change the amount each heir will inherit.

ESTATE/INHERITANCE TAXES You need to determine whether the location of the initial procedure will have an impact on the amount of taxes that need to be paid.

THE MISSING WILL

People tend to put off making a Will until they think they need to. For many, that need arises when they are elderly and/or seriously ill and have property that they want to leave to someone. It is uncommon for a young person to have a Will; but those who are aged, and with significant assets, usually have one.

A survey conducted for the American Association of Retired Persons ("AARP") found that the probability of having a Will increases with age. Forty-four percent of those surveyed who were between the ages of 50 to 54 had a Will. This increased to 85% for those 80 and older. You can find details of the survey at the AARP Web site.

 AARP WEB SITE
http://research.aarp.org

Those who make a Will, usually tell the person who they appoint as Executor, of the existence of the Will. Chances are, that someone in the decedent's circle of family and friends, knows whether there is a Will. If you believe that the decedent had a Will, but you cannot find it, then there are at least three places to check out:

⇨ THE DECEDENT'S ATTORNEY

Look at the decedent's checkbook for the past few years and see whether he paid any attorney fees. If you are able to locate the decedent's attorney, then call and inquire whether the attorney ever drafted a Will for the decedent, and if so, whether the attorney has the original Will in his possession. If the attorney has the original Will, then ask the attorney to forward the Will to the Clerk of the Probate Court. Asking the attorney to forward the Will to the Court does not obligate you to employ the attorney should you later find that Probate is necessary.

⇨ **THE DECEDENT'S SAFE DEPOSIT BOX**

If you believe that the decedent had a Will but you cannot find it, then check to see if the decedent had a safe deposit box. If he did, you will need to gain entry to that box to see whether the Will is in the box. See the next page for an explanation of how to gain entry to the safe deposit box.

⇨ **THE REGISTER OF PROBATE**

Massachusetts law gives residents the right to deposit their Will with the Register of Probate in the county of their residence and name someone who is to be given the Will should the Will maker die. When the Will is deposited, the Register gives the Will maker a Certificate of Receipt. If you come across the Certificate, you can contact the Register of Probate and arrange to have the Will admitted to Probate. Even without findings a Certificate of Receipt, it is a good idea to check with the Register. It may be that the Certificate, and not the Will, is lost. If the decedent lived in other counties in Massachusetts during his lifetime, then check with the Register in each of those counties (MGL 191:10).

If the Will was deposited and no one claims it, then once the Register receives notice of the death, the Register will give it to the Probate Court, and the Will be publicly opened during the next Court session (MGL 191:12).

 **A COPY AND NO ORIGINAL**

If you have a copy of the Will, but cannot locate the original, the Court will allow the copy into Probate provided you can prove that the document is a true copy of the decedent's valid, unrevoked Will (MGL 192:10). You will need to employ an attorney who is experienced in Probate matters to present such proof to the Court.

ACCESSING THE SAFE DEPOSIT BOX

When a person leases a safe deposit box, the bank, or leasing company, has the person sign an agreement that explains who is allowed access to the box. If the decedent had a safe deposit box that he leased jointly with another, then the agreement usually states that each joint tenant has free access to the box. With such arrangement should one joint tenant become incapacitated or die, the surviving joint tenant is free to go to the safe deposit box and withdraw any or all of the contents of the box.

A safe deposit box leased in the decedent's name only is a different matter. Unless the agreement with the bank states that another person has access to the contents upon the death or incapacity of the decedent, no one can gain entry to the safe deposit box other than a Court appointed Personal Representative.

It may be no Probate procedure is necessary and that the only thing in the safe deposit box is the decedent's original Will. If you suspect that this to be the case, you can ask the bank to allow you to inspect the contents of the box, in the presence of a bank or company official, to see if the Will is there.

If they allow the inspection and a Will is found, you can ask them to forward the Will to the Probate Court. If they agree, then ask them to make a copy of the Will for you in the event the original gets lost in transit.

If you need to gain entry to a safe deposit box held in the decedent's name only, it is a good idea to first call the bank, and ask them to explain their company policy to you. If they agree to allow you to inspect the contents of the box, then ask what identification they will require of you. Many companies require that you show them personal identification, such as your driver's license, and a certified copy of the death certificate.

If the bank will allow inspection of the contents of the box only upon Court order, then some sort of Probate procedure will be necessary. If you believe that the decedent had few assets, it may be possible to have a Temporary Representative appointed to gain access to the safe deposit box, rather than begin a full Probate procedure.

Chapter 6 explains the different Probate procedures that are available to you in Massachusetts. But before we discuss the different kinds of Probate procedure, we need to determine what bills need to be paid (the topic of the next chapter) and who is entitled to inherit the decedent's property (the topic of Chapter 5).

What Bills Need To Be Paid? 4

The Personal Representative has the duty to be sure that all valid claims against the Estate are paid. If the decedent had debts, but no money or property, then of course, there is no way to pay the claim. The only remaining question is whether anyone else is responsible to pay the decedent's debts. If the decedent was married, then the first person the creditor will look to, is the decedent's spouse. To understand the basis of this expectation, you need to know a bit of the history of our legal system.

Our laws are derived from English Common Law. Under early English Common Law, a single woman had the right to own property in her own name and also the right to contract to buy or sell property; but when she married, her legal identity merged with her spouse. She could not hold property free from her husband's claim or control. She could no longer enter into a contract without her husband's permission.

Once married, a woman became financially dependent on her husband. He, in turn, became legally responsible to provide his wife with basic necessities — food, clothing, shelter and medical services. If anyone provided basic necessities to his wife, then, regardless of whether the husband agreed to be responsible for the debt, he became obliged to pay for them. This law was called the DOCTRINE OF NECESSARIES.

States in America departed from English Common Law by enacting a series of Married Women's Rights Acts giving a married woman the right town property and to contract in her own name.

Judges had to decide:

If a wife can own property and contract to pay for her own necessities, should her husband be responsible for such debts in the event she does not have enough money to pay for them?

For those states deciding to continue to hold the husband liable, a second question to be decided was:

If the husband is responsible for his wife's necessities, should she be responsible for his?

In some states, notably Florida, courts decided that neither partner was responsible to pay the other's necessities, unless they contracted or agreed to do so. But in Massachusetts they came to a different conclusion.

The Massachusetts legislature passed laws stating that a woman has the right to own property, but a husband continues to be responsible to pay for his wife and family's necessities. Either party can purchase necessities for the family. If the contracting spouse does not have sufficient funds to pay for these items, the debt must be paid from property they hold together as husband and wife.

If there is no joint property, the husband remains liable for the debt from his **separate** property; i.e., property that he owned prior to the marriage and that has not been co-mingled with marital property. The wife is liable for necessities purchased for the family from her separate property, but only if she knew or consented to the purchase, and she has at least $2,000 as her own separate property. Even if the wife is liable, under Massachusetts law that liability is limited to $100 per purchase of a necessity (MGL 209:1, 209:2, 209:7).

JOINT DEBTS

A *joint debt* is a debt that two or more people are responsible to pay. Usually the contract or promissory note reads that the parties agree to *joint and several liability*, meaning they all agree to pay the debt and each of them agree to be personally responsible to pay the debt. A joint debt can also be in the form of monies owed by one person with payment guaranteed by another person. If the person who owes the money does not pay, then the *guarantor* (the person who guaranteed payment) is responsible to make payment.

Hospital bills, nursing home bills, funeral expenses, legal fees to Probate the decedent's Estate, are all debts of his Estate. They are not joint debts unless someone guaranteed payment for the monies owed.

THE ESTATE MUST PAY FOR JOINT DEBTS

If the decedent and another were jointly responsible for monies owed, then Massachusetts law provides that the debt must be paid from the decedent's Estate as if the contract (or judgment) were joint and severable, or as if the judgment were against the decedent alone (MGL 197:8). Of course if there are insufficient funds in the Estate to pay the joint debt, then the joint debtor remains liable to pay for the debt.

 **SPOUSE**   JOINT SPOUSAL DEBTS

Loans signed by the decedent and his spouse are joint debts, as are charges on credit cards that both were authorized to use. Property taxes are a joint debt if the decedent and the spouse both owned the property. All of these debts can be paid from the decedent's Estate.

Suppose all of the decedent's funds are held jointly with his spouse or a family member and the joint owner of the account did not agree to pay those debts. Can the creditor require that half of the joint funds be set aside to pay the debt?

The answer to this question depends on how the joint property is titled. As we will see in Chapter 5 there are different ways to hold property jointly with another. Massachusetts courts have ruled that property held *jointly with rights of survivorship*, belongs to the surviving joint owner as of the date of death and it is not available to pay the decedent's debts (*Weaver vs. New Bedford*, 335 Mass. 644 (1957)).

BUT NOT EXEMPT FROM UNCLE SAM

Bank accounts in the name of two or more persons with rights of survivorship, are payable to the surviving joint owner(s) (MGL 167D:5). The surviving owners have no obligation to use the joint account funds to pay the decedent's creditors because the funds are not part of the decedent's **Probate Estate**. However, the decedent's share of the joint account is included as part of the decedent's **Taxable Estate**. If Estate Taxes are due to the federal or state government and there no other funds to pay those taxes, the remaining owners of the joint account will need to contribute as much of the decedent's share of the account as is necessary to pay the tax bill (MGL 65A:5).

NO MONEY — NO PROPERTY

If the decedent owed money then the debt needs to be paid from assets owned by the decedent — which leads to the next question "Did the decedent have any money in his own name when he died?"

If the decedent died without any money or property in his name, then there is no money to pay any creditor. The only question that remains is whether anyone else is liable to pay those bills. The issue of payment most often arises in relation to services provided by nursing homes. When a person enters a nursing home, he is usually too ill to speak for himself or even sign his name. In such cases, the nursing home administrator will ask the spouse or a family member to sign a battery of papers on behalf of the patient before allowing the patient to enter the facility.

Buried in that battery of papers may be a statement that the family member agrees to be responsible for payment to the nursing home. If the family member refuses to guarantee payment and the patient's finances are limited, the facility may refuse to admit the patient.

Under the Federal Nursing Home Reform Law, a nursing home that accepts Medicare or Medicaid payments is prohibited from requiring a family member to guarantee payment as a condition of allowing the patient to enter that facility (USC Title 42 §1395I-3(c)(5)(A)(ii)). Nonetheless, it is common practice for a nursing home, in effect, to say "Either someone agrees to pay for the patient's bill or you need to find a different facility."

If the patient is a married man, with no assets in his name or held jointly with his spouse, then the facility will ask his spouse to be fully liable for the payment of his care. Even if the spouse agrees to pay, under Massachusetts law, the most that the nursing home may be able to collect from the wife is $100 (MGL 209:1, 209:2, 209:7). See page 82.

For an insolvent patient, the solution to the problem is to have the patient admitted to a facility as a Medicaid patient. If the patient enters as a private paying resident, and then runs out of money, the nursing home has the right to transfer or discharge him from their facility, provided they inform the patient or his next of kin, of that right when he entered the facility (940 Code of Massachusetts Regulations 4.02).

But suppose the decedent had some money when he entered the nursing home and a family member (other than his spouse) agreed to guarantee payment for his stay. Is that family member now liable to pay the decedent's final nursing home bill if he died without funds?

An experienced Elder Law attorney will be able to answer that question after examining the documents that were signed and the conditions under which the patient entered the nursing home. In particular, the attorney will want to know whether the family member was coerced into signing as a guarantor, and whether he was fully informed of his liabilities under that contract.

PAYING THE DECEDENT'S BILLS

If the decedent owed money and he died owning property belonging to him alone, such as a bank account, securities, or real property, then there may be money available to pay monies owed by the decedent. It is up to the decedent's Personal Representative to pay all valid debts, but to do so the Personal Representative first must gain possession of the decedent's assets. To get possession of the decedent's assets, there will need to be a Probate procedure to determine who is entitled to the decedent's property.

Once the Probate procedure begins, all of the decedent's creditors will be given an opportunity to come forward and produce evidence showing how much is owed. The Personal Representative needs to look over each unpaid invoice and decide whether it is a valid bill. The problem with making that decision is that the decedent is not here to say whether he actually received the goods and services now being billed to his Estate.

That is especially the case for medical or nursing care bills. An example of improper billing brought to the attention of this author was that of a bill submitted for a physical examination of the decedent. The bill listed the date of the examination as July 10th, but the decedent died on July 9th. Other incorrect billings may not be as obvious, so each invoice needs to be carefully examined.

If the Personal Representative decides to challenge a bill, and is unable to settle the matter with the creditor, then the Probate Court will decide whether the debt is valid and should be paid.

MEDICAL BILLS COVERED BY INSURANCE

If the decedent had health insurance you may receive an invoice stamped "THIS IS NOT A BILL." This means the health care provider has submitted the bill to the decedent's health insurance company and expects to be paid by them. If the decedent was receiving Medicare, you will receive a *Medicare Summary Notice* listing all of the services or supplies that were billed to Medicare for the prior 30 days. In some areas of the country, you can get a copy of the decedent's Medicare Summary Notice from the Internet: http://www.medicare.gov

Even though payment is not requested, it is important to verify that the bill is valid for two reasons:

➤ LATER LIABILITY

If the insurer refuses to pay the claim, the facility will seek payment from whoever is in possession of the decedent's property, and that may reduce the amount inherited by the beneficiaries.

➤ INCREASED HEALTH CARE COSTS

Regardless of whether the decedent was covered by a private health care insurer or Medicare, improper billing increases the cost of health insurance to all of us. Consumers pay high premiums for health coverage. We, as taxpayers, all share the cost of Medicare. If unnecessary or fraudulent billing is not checked, then ultimately, we all pay.

If you believe that you have come across a case of Medicare fraud, you can call the ANTI-FRAUD HOTLINE (800) 447-8477 and report the incident to the Office of the Inspector General of the United States Department of Health and Human Services.

HOW TO CHECK MEDICARE BILLING

The structure of Medicare has been changed giving people in some parts of the country, the option of staying with the *Original Medicare Plan* or choosing one of the *Medicare + Choice Plans*. Health care coverage depends on which plan is chosen. If the decedent was covered by Medicare, you need to determine whether he was covered under the Original Medicare Plan, or whether he chose a Medicare + Choice Plan. The publication MEDICARE AND YOU explains coverage under the different options. See page 49 to obtain a copy of the booklet. Coverage under Medicare + Choice Plans is explained in the membership materials given to the decedent at the time he signed up for the plan.

BILLING UNDER THE ORIGINAL MEDICARE PLAN

An important billing question for those under the Original Medicare Plan is whether the health care provider agreed to accept Medicare *assignment*, meaning that they agreed to accept the Medicare-approved amount. If so, the patient is responsible for the coinsurance rate (usually 20% of the approved amount) and any deductible amount. Doctors and health care providers who do not accept assignment, are limited in the amount they can charge for a Medicare covered service. The highest they can charge is **15%** over the Medicare-approved amount. This *Limiting Charge* applies only to certain services and does not apply to supplies and equipment.

For those who are in the Original Medicare Plan, a doctor or a supplier may give notice saying that Medicare probably will not pay for the service that is about to be provided. This is called an *Advance Beneficiary Notice*. If the patient still wants the service after receiving such Notice, he will be asked to sign an agreement stating that he will pay for the service, in the event that Medicare does not pay.

If all of this appears confusing, it is.

To check the decedent's Medicare billing, you need the answers to the following questions:

What is the plan?

Determine whether the decedent was in the Original Medicare Plan or in one of the Medicare + Choice Plans.

What is covered under the plan?

The *Medicare and You* booklet explains what is covered under the Original Medicare Plan. You will need a copy of the membership materials for the Medicare + Choice Plans to determine what is covered under that plan.

Does the Provider accept Assignment?

If the decedent was in the Original Medicare Plan, you need to determine whether the health care provider accepted assignment; and if not whether the Limiting Charge applies to the services provided. If assignment is accepted or the Limiting Charge applies, you need to determine the Medicare-approved amount.

Did the decedent agree to pay?

If the decedent was in the Original Medicare Plan, check to see whether the decedent was given an Advance Beneficiary Notice; and if so, whether he signed a contract agreeing to pay in the event that Medicare refuses to pay.

DENIAL OF
MEDICARE COVERAGE

If the health care provider reports to you that a service provided to the decedent is not covered by Medicare, or if the facility submits the bill to Medicare and Medicare refuses to pay, then check to see if you agree with that ruling by finding answers to the questions on the prior page. If you believe that the decedent was wrongly denied coverage, then you can appeal that decision.

If the decedent was in the Original Medicare Plan, you will find information about how to file an appeal on the Medicare Summary Notice. If he was part of the Medicare + Choice Plan, you will find that information in his health care plan materials.

GETTING HELP WITH THE APPEAL

If you believe that the decedent was wrongly denied coverage, then you can appeal that decision. The Greater Boston Legal Services helps people with their Medicare appeal. You can call them at (800) 323-3205.

If you want a local attorney to assist with your appeal, you can call the Massachusetts Bar to refer you to an attorney experienced in Medicare appeals. Some attorneys work *pro bono* (literally for the public good; i.e. without charge) but most charge to assist in an appeal. Federal statute 42 U.S.C. §406(a)(2)(A) limits the amount an attorney may charge for a successful Medicare appeal to 25% of the amount recovered or $4,000, whichever is the smaller amount.

Medicaid is a program that provides medical and long term nursing care for people with low income and limited resources. In Massachusetts, it is called *MassHealth*. The program is funded jointly by the federal and state government. Federal law requires the state to recover monies spent from the Estate of a Medicaid recipient who was 55 or older when the decedent received Medicaid assistance. The state will seek reimbursement for the cost of nursing home care or for home based care or for other community based services. Both state and federal law prohibits any recovery of monies spent, until the surviving spouse, and/or disabled child of the decedent are deceased (42 U.S.C. 1396(p), MGL 118E:31).

Usually there is no money to recover because to qualify for MassHealth, a person may not have more than $2,000 in assets. But sometimes it happens that person on Medicaid dies and his Estate later receives money perhaps as part of a settlement of a lawsuit. Also it could happen that the decedent owned his home. Owing a home does not disqualify a person from receiving MassHealth, however once he dies the state has the right to place a lien on that home and seek recovery from the proceeds of the sale of the house. The Personal Representative is required to send notice to the Massachusetts Division of Medical Assistance and give them an opportunity to file a claim against the Estate. If the Personal Representative fails to give notice, whoever inherits the property will be liable to Division up to the amount they inherited (MGL 118E:32).

SOME THINGS ARE CREDITOR PROOF

Sometimes it happens that the decedent had money or property titled in his name only, but he also had a significant amount of debt. In such cases the beneficiaries may wonder whether they should go through a Probate procedure if there will be little, if anything, left after the creditors are paid. Before making the decision consider that some assets are protected under Massachusetts law:

✧ HOUSEHOLD ITEMS ✧

If the decedent lived with his family at the time of his death, then several items can be kept by the family free of the decedent's (or their) debt including:

⇨ household furniture, up to $3,000 in value;

⇨ an automobile necessary for personal transportation or to maintain employment up to $700 in value;

⇨ Provisions (food, household items) for the family use up to $300 in value

⇨ Bible, school books and library up to $200 in value;

⇨ one sewing machine, in actual use by the family up to $200 in value (MGL 235:34).

NECESSITIES FOR SPOUSE/MINOR CHILD

The Probate Court can set aside the decedent's personal property as being necessary for the surviving spouse and/or minor child to use. If there is no spouse, then up to $100 can be set aside for each minor child. This personal property is taken free of the cost of the Probate Administration and free of the decedent's debts (MGL 196:2).

✧ THE HOMESTEAD ✧

Massachusetts property registered by the decedent as an Estate of Homestead has up to $300,000 creditor protection during his lifetime. This creditor protection continues if the decedent is survived by a spouse or minor child. Specifically, if the amount owed by the decedent is less than the value of the his creditor protection, then the creditor cannot require that the homestead be sold to pay for those debts, provided the homestead continues to be occupied by the decedent's minor child or surviving spouse. If there is a child and no spouse, creditor protection is lost once the child reaches 18. If there is a surviving spouse, creditor protection continues until the surviving spouse remarries or dies.

Creditor protection also continues if the decedent owned the homestead jointly with another person (not necessarily spouse or child), and that person continues to occupy the property as his homestead. The surviving owner may need to apply for his own Estate of Homestead by signing a Declaration and filing it with the Registry of Deeds in the county where the property is located (see Page 35).

EXCEPTIONS TO THE RULE

Creditor protection does not extend to taxes, delinquent payments for child or spousal support, monies owed prior to acquiring the homestead, mortgages or mechanics' liens on the property. It also does not extend to judgments against the decedent that involve fraud, undue influence, mistake, duress or lack of capacity. And of course, if the decedent was the sole owner of the property and not survived by spouse or minor child, creditor protection ends upon his death and the homestead can be sold to pay for monies owed by the decedent (MGL 188:1; 188:2, 188:4).

✧ GROUP INSURANCE PROCEEDS ✧

If the decedent had a group annuity contract or a group life insurance policy as part of his employment, then the proceeds of such policies are creditor proof. The insurance proceeds are paid to the beneficiary of the policy free of the decedent's debt, with the exception of monies owed by the decedent for child or spousal support. If the decedent owed back support, then the proceeds of the policy may need to be used to pay for those debts (MGL 175:132C, 175:135).

✧ LIFE INSURANCE PROCEEDS ✧

The beneficiary of a life insurance policy takes the proceeds free of the monies owed by the decedent, and this is so regardless of the value of the insurance policy. The only exception is the purchase of a policy to defraud creditors. For example, suppose the decedent owed a large sum of money and instead of paying the debt, he used that sum to purchase a life insurance policy. If the creditor can prove that the purpose of the purchase was to avoid paying the debt, then the money paid by the decedent for the policy, plus interest on that money, must be paid to the creditors from the proceeds of the policy (MGL 175:125).

NO CREDITOR PROTECTION FOR DECEDENT'S ESTATE

The proceeds of a group insurance policy and a life insurance policy are creditor proof provided the beneficiary of the policy is not the decedent's Estate. For example, suppose a person names his son as the primary beneficiary of the policy, and himself as the alternate beneficiary. If the son dies before the father, then the money goes to the father's Estate, and in that case, the proceeds of the policy are available to pay monies owed by the decedent father.

✧ PENSION PLANS ✧

Annuities, pensions, profit sharing or other retirement plans regulated by the federal Employee Retirement Income Security Act of 1974, including Keogh plans, and plans identified by the Internal Revenue Code of 1986 as 401(a) and 403(b) (including IRA accounts) are creditor proof. Monies received by a beneficiary of such plans are protected from the decedent's creditors with two exceptions:

SUPPORT PAYMENTS

Pensions funds can be used to pay monies owed by the decedent for back child or spousal support (MGL 235:34A)

NO EXEMPTION FOR TAXES

In general, income taxes are not paid when money is placed in a retirement plan. Taxes are paid when the monies are withdrawn from the account regardless of whether the monies are withdrawn by the retiree or the person named as beneficiary of the retirement plan. If you are inheriting money from the decedent's pension, annuity or retirement allowance, then you may need to pay taxes on those monies. You should to consult with an attorney or an accountant to determine how much money needs to be set aside to pay for federal and state income taxes.

✧ BENEFITS FROM A FRATERNAL BENEFIT SOCIETY ✧

Any benefit that is payable by a fraternal benefit society (e.g., AARP, American Legion, Kiwanis, Lighthouse for the Blind, Rotary Club, etc.) is free of the monies owed by the decedent. In fact, benefits paid by a fraternal benefit society are free from the claims of the creditors of the member of the society AND from the creditors of the beneficiary (MGL 176:22).

✧ THERE IS A PRIORITY OF PAYMENT ✧

Next to consider is that not all Probate debts are equal. Massachusetts Statute establishes an order of priority for payment of claims made against the decedent's Estate:

FUNERAL EXPENSES AND COST OF ADMINISTRATION

The necessary expenses of the decedent's funeral, the cost of his last sickness and the cost of the Probate procedure, (including attorney's fees and fees charged by the Personal Representative) must be satisfied before any other debt can be paid. If Estate monies are left once these bills are paid, then claims are paid in the following order:

CLASS 1: FEDERAL TAXES

If monies or taxes are owed by the decedent to the federal government, and the monies owed have preference under federal law, then these debts have top priority.

CLASS 2: STATE TAXES AND CHILD SUPPORT

Monies owed to Massachusetts for taxes, and back child support payments are second in priority.

CLASS 3: REPAYMENT FOR STATE ASSISTANCE

Medicaid benefits for nursing care provided to the decedent after age 55 are reimbursable to the Massachusetts Division of Medical Assistance as a Class 3 debt; provided the decedent is not survived by a spouse or disabled child.

CLASS 4: PAYMENT TO DECEDENT'S EMPLOYEE

Up to $100 of monies owed to an employee of the decedent for work performed within a year of his death, is 4th in line for payment.

CLASS 5: PAYMENT FOR NECESSITIES

Fifth in line is payment (up to $100) for necessities provided to the decedent or his family within 6 months of his death.

CLASS 6:   ALL OTHER DEBTS

If the Personal Representative determines that there is not sufficient money to pay all of the claims against the Estate, then he will report that fact to the Probate Court. The Court may then decide to appoint two or more *Commissioners* whose job it will be to examine all of the claims against the Estate and present a list of the claims and the amounts owed, to the Court.

The Commissioners will set a time and place to receive all claims against the Estate. Notice will be sent to all known creditors to submit their claims to the Commissioners.

If the Court does not appoint any Commissioner, then the Court will instruct the Personal Representative to give notice to the creditors of the time and place where their claims will be examined.

Once the claims are submitted, the Court will order payment. If there are insufficient funds to pay creditors in a given class, the Court will order that the monies be prorated between the creditors in that class. No payment will be made to creditors in a given class until creditors in the prior class have been paid (MGL 198:1, 198:2, 198:3, 198:4, 198:5).

✧ THERE IS A STATUTE OF LIMITATIONS ✧

Finally, consider that there is a statute of limitations for bringing a claim against the Probate Estate of the decedent. If a creditor fails to properly serve the Personal Representative with notice of the a claim within one year from the date of death, then that claim cannot be enforced against the Personal Representative.

It could happen that there is a valid reason for the delay of a creditor in filing a claim. In such case, the Court might allow a claim filed after a year. If the Estate is still open, the claim can be paid from the decedent's Estate, but not from monies that were distributed to the beneficiaries before the creditor filed his claim (MGL 197:9, 197:10).

There are exceptions to the year limit such as mortgages, federal claims, and monies owed to the Division for public assistance that was provided to the decedent (MGL 118E:32). But, in general, if no one begins a Probate procedure for a year, then the beneficiaries may be able to obtain possession of the decedent's assets free from creditor claims.

Some may be thinking that it may be a good idea to postpone Probate until a year has passed.

Read on before you decide to wait out the year.

DECEDENT LEAVING CONSIDERABLE DEBT

If the decedent died leaving much debt and no property, then the solution is simple. No Probate, no one gets paid. But if the decedent had property and died owing a significant amount of money, his heirs may be tempted to wait the year and begin Probate at that time. Such strategy may turn out to be more hassle than its worth. Some creditors are tenacious and will use whatever legal strategy is available in order to be paid. For example, if no one starts a Probate procedure, anytime after 30 days from the date of death, a creditor can petition the Court to be appointed as Personal Representative of the Estate. If the decedent owed taxes, and no one starts the Probate procedure, the Commissioner of Revenue has four months from the date of death to ask the Court to appoint someone to administer the Estate (MGL 193:3, 193:7).

As we will see in Chapter 6, a Personal Representative has much authority when conducting a Probate proceeding. Family members may object to having a creditor as a Personal Representative, so there could be a court battle over who has priority to be appointed as Personal Representative. Court battles are expensive, emotionally as well as financially. Before you decide to wait out a creditor by postponing Probate for a year, consult with an attorney who is experienced in Probate matters for an opinion about the best way to administer the Estate.

MONIES OWED TO THE DECEDENT

Suppose you owed money to the decedent. Do you need to pay that debt now that he is dead? That depends on whether there is some written document that says the debt is forgiven once the decedent dies. For example, suppose you borrowed money from the decedent to buy your home. If he left a Will saying that once he dies, your debt is forgiven, then you do not need to make any more payments. If you signed a promissory note and mortgage at the time you borrowed the money from the decedent, then the Personal Representative should sign the original promissory note PAID IN FULL and return the note to you. If the mortgage was recorded, the Personal Representative should sign and record a satisfaction of mortgage.

If you owed money to the decedent and there is no Will, or if there is a Will, and no mention of forgiving the debt, then you still owe the money. Monies borrowed from the decedent and his spouse need to be repaid to the spouse. Monies borrowed from the decedent only, become an asset to the Estate of the decedent, meaning that you owe the money to the decedent's Estate. If you are one of the beneficiaries of the Estate, you can deduct the money from your inheritance.

For example, suppose your father left $70,000 in a bank account to be divided equally between you and your two brothers. If you owed your father $20,000, then your father's Estate is really worth $90,000. Instead of paying the $20,000, you can agree to receive $10,000 and have the $20,000 debt forgiven. Each of your brothers will then receive $30,000 in cash.

Who Are The Beneficiaries? 5

A question that comes up early on is who is entitled to the property of the decedent. To answer the question you first need to know how the property was titled (owned) as of the date of death.

There are three ways to own property. The decedent could have owned property jointly with another person; or in trust for another person; or the decedent could have owned property titled in his name only.

In general, upon the decedent's death:

Joint Property belongs to the surviving joint owner.

Trust Property belongs to the beneficiary
of the Trust.

Property owned by the **decedent only** is inherited
by the beneficiaries named in the Will.
If there is no Will, then the property goes to his heirs
according to the Massachusetts
Laws of Descent and Distribution.

NOTE ⇨ If the decedent was married, then his
spouse may have rights in his property.

This chapter describes each type of ownership in detail.

PROPERTY OWNED JOINTLY

Bank accounts, securities, motor vehicles, real property can all be owned jointly by two or more people. If one of the joint owners dies, then the survivor(s) continue to own their share of the property. Who owns the share belonging to the decedent depends on how the joint ownership was set up.

THE JOINT BANK ACCOUNT

When a bank account is opened the depositors sign an agreement with the bank that states the term and conditions of the account. If the account is opened in two or more names, the contract will say whether each depositor has authority to make a withdrawal, or whether two signatures are necessary. Unless the account states differently, in Massachusetts, a joint account is a *survivorship* account, meaning that should one joint owner die, the account is owned by the remaining owner(s). Each owner of a joint account has free access to the monies in the account and can withdraw all of the monies in the account.

If a survivorship account is held in three names and one owner dies, either of the survivors can go to the bank and withdraw all of the funds in the account. With such an arrangement, the surviving owners need to cooperate with each other to divide the funds in the account fairly (MGL 167D:5).

JOINTLY OWNED SECURITIES

You can determine whether the decedent owns a security alone or jointly with another by examining the face of the stock or bond certificate. If two names are printed on the certificate followed by a statement that the owners are "joint tenants with rights of survivorship ("JTWRS")," or if married, as husband and wife, or as "Tenants By The Entireties" or simply as "Joint Tenants," then the surviving owner can either cash in the security or ask the company to issue a new certificate in the name of the surviving owner.

A security held jointly without rights of survivorship, is held as a *Tenancy In Common.* Should one co-owner die, his share goes to whomever he named as beneficiary of his Will, or if no Will, it goes to his heirs as determined by the Massachusetts Laws of Descent and Distribution. Those laws are explained later in this Chapter.

Each state has its own securities regulations. If a security held in two or more names, was registered or purchased in another state, you will need to contact the company to determine how the account was set up; i.e., with or without rights of survivorship.

If the decedent held his securities in a brokerage account, then the name of the owner of that account is printed on the monthly or quarterly brokerage statement. Not all brokerage firms print the name of a joint owner on the brokerage statement, so you need to contact the firm to determine whether there is a surviving joint owner, or perhaps a beneficiary of the account. Request a copy of the contract that is the basis of the account. The contract will show when the account was opened and the terms of the brokerage account.

If a motor vehicle is held jointly, the name of each owner is printed on the title to the motor vehicle as Owner 1 and Owner 2. If the two owners are married, then when one spouse dies, the other owns the car without the need for any Probate procedure. If the owners are not married, a Personal Representative will need to be appointed to have the car transferred to the surviving owner, or to whoever the decedent named as the beneficiary of the decedent's "half"of the car. We explain how to transfer the car in Chapter 6.

SPOUSE ━━━ CAR IN DECEDENT'S NAME ONLY

If the decedent was married and the family car in his name only, then unless he left the car to someone in his Will, the car goes to the surviving spouse. All the spouse need do to transfer title is go to the Registry of Motor Vehicles and sign an ***Affidavit*** (a written statement, sworn to before a notary public) stating that the decedent did not make a gift of the car in his Will (MGL 90D:15A).

If the decedent was single and died without a Will, then the car goes to the next of kin as defined in Massachusetts's Laws of Descent and Distribution.

The name of the owner of real property is printed on the face of the deed. To determine whether the decedent owned the property jointly with another person, you need to look at the last recorded deed. See Chapter 3 if you cannot locate the deed..

> ## WARRANTY DEED
>
> ROBERT TRAYNOR, a single man,
> of Essex County, Massachusetts,
> for consideration of $120,000, paid
> grants to JAMES CODY, a married man
> and JAMES CODY, JR. a single man,
> as **JOINT TENANTS**,
> of Suffolk County, Massachusetts,
> with warranty covenants . . .
> the land in Suffolk County
> with legal description
>
> . . .

Robert Traynor is the *Grantor* of the deed. That means he transferred the property to James Cody and James Cody, Jr. who are the *Grantees* and present owners of the property. The Grantees own the property as *joint tenants*, meaning that should one of them die, the surviving joint tenant owns the property 100%. Nothing need be done to establish the ownership, however the decedent's name remains on the deed.

If you are the surviving joint owner of real property you may want to have an Affidavit recorded in the Registry of Deeds stating that the joint owner has died, and that you are now the sole owner (MGL 183:5A). See Chapter 6 for an explanation of how to record the Affidavit.

📋 DEED HELD AS TENANTS IN COMMON

If the deed identifies the decedent and another as TENANTS IN COMMON, then there are no rights of survivorship. Each person owns his own share of the property. Unless the deed says differently, each Tenant In Common owns an equal share. The decedent's share of property held as a Tenant In Common, goes to the beneficiary of his Will. If the decedent died without a Will, then the Laws of Descent and Distribution determine who now owns the decedent's share. A Probate procedure will be necessary in order to transfer the decedent's share of a Tenancy In Common to the new owner.

NO SURVIVORSHIP UNLESS STATED IN THE DEED

A deed to two or more people is a Tenancy In Common unless the deed specifically indicates a joint tenancy. For example, there are rights of survivorship if the Grantees are identified as:

"Harold Krol **jointly** with William Krol"

or

"Harold Krol and William Krol in **Joint Tenancy**"

or

"Harold Krol and William Krol **or the Survivor**."

But a deed to "Harold Krol and William Krol" without any indication of survivorship, is a Tenancy In Common (MGL 184:7).

Best to consult with an attorney if there is any question about how to interpret the deed.

🗎 DEED WITH A LIFE ESTATE

A *Life Estate* interest in real property means that the person who owns the Life Estate has the right to live in that property until he dies. You can identify a Life Estate interest by examining the face of the deed. If somewhere on the face of the deed you see the phrase RESERVING A LIFE ESTATE to the deceased Grantor, then the Grantee(s) now own the property. For example, suppose the granting paragraph of the deed reads:

> ROSE REILLY, a single woman,
> of Franklin County, Massachusetts,
> for nominal non-monetary consideration,
> grants to PETER REILLY, a married man
> of Norfolk County, Massachusetts,
> RESERVING A LIFE ESTATE TO THE GRANTOR
>
> . . .

Rose is the owner of the Life Estate. Peter owns the *Remainder Interest* in the property. Peter has no right to occupy the property during Rose's lifetime, but once she dies, he will own the property 100%. He will be free to take possession of the property or transfer it, as he sees fit.

As with a Joint Tenancy, nothing need be done to establish Peter's ownership of the property, however he may want to have his attorney record an Affidavit and death certificate so that anyone who examines title to the property will know that the owner of the Life Estate is deceased, and Peter is now the sole owner. See Chapter 6 for a discussion of the transfer of title to real property.

🗎 DEED HELD AS HUSBAND AND WIFE

There are rights of survivorship if a husband and wife own real property as Joint Tenants or as **Tenants By The Entirety.** Should one of the parties die, the surviving spouse will own the property 100%. Again, nothing need be done to establish that ownership, however the surviving spouse may want to have an Affidavit recorded with the Registry of Deeds (MGL 183:5A).

RIGHTS OF THE SPOUSE

If the decedent held real property in his name only, then the surviving spouse may have rights in that property. In Massachusetts, the surviving spouse has Dower rights of a one-third Life Estate interest in real property owned by the decedent.

Dower rights are not automatic. Those rights must be asserted within six months from the date the Personal Representative is authorized to act, or else they are *waived* (given up) (MGL 189:1).

If the decedent owned an Estate of Homestead, then the surviving spouse also has rights in that property as explained on the next page.

SPOUSE ➤ AN INVISIBLE LIFE ESTATE

If the decedent had an Estate Of Homestead, then the surviving spouse can continue to live in the premises until she remarries or dies. If there is no spouse but a minor child, then the child can live there until he reaches the age of 18. The surviving spouse owns a Life Estate interest in the home, regardless of whether the decedent owned the property in his name only, or jointly with another, or as a Tenant-In-Common; and regardless of whether the decedent's Will gives the home to someone who is not his spouse (MGL 188:1, 188:4).

An Estate of Homestead can be created in one of two ways. When the property is purchased, the decedent could have had the deed identify the property as Homestead property, or he could have recorded a Declaration of Homestead with the Registry of Deeds. Either way, the Registry of Deeds, in the county where the property is located, has a record of whether there is an Estate of Homestead. A mobile home can be held as an Estate of Homestead by filing a Declaration of Homestead with the city or town Clerk's office in the city or town where the mobile home is located (MGL 188:2).

An Estate of Homestead can be terminated by having the owner and his spouse deed the property to another or they can sign a release and record it in the Registry of Deeds where the property is located (MGL 188:7). An examination of title to the property will reveal whether a release of Homestead has been recorded.

 **LAWYER** | DIVORCED PRIOR TO DEATH

As soon as a couple is divorced, all dower rights are extinguished. The decedent's former spouse cannot make a claim of dower's rights to property held in the decedent's name only (MGL 208:27). If the decedent and his former spouse owned real property as joint tenants, the Final Judgment should state who owns the property after the divorce.

If the deed to the property owned by the decedent has not been transferred according to the Final Judgment, you need to consult with an attorney to have a new deed prepared that identifies the new owners of the property.

 This discussion on the different types of ownership of real property assumes that you are in possession of the most recent, valid deed. The decedent could have signed another, later, deed. Before you come to a conclusion about who inherits the property it is advisable have an attorney do a title search to determine the owner of the property as of the decedent's date of death.

 **LAWYER**　　THE OUT OF STATE DEED

The laws of the state or country where the property is located determine who inherits property in that state. If the decedent owned property in another state or country, then even if the decedent was a resident of Massachusetts, the laws of the state or country where the property is located determine who inherits property in that state.

The laws of each state are similar, but not the same. In Massachusetts, property held as Joint Tenants means that there are Rights of Survivorship; but in other states, such as Alabama, property held jointly is a Tenancy In Common unless the deed specifically states that there is a Right of Survivorship.

In some states, such as Florida, just the fact that deed identifies the couple as being married is sufficient to create a Tenancy By The Entirety.

If the decedent owned property in another state, it is important to consult with an attorney in that state to determine who now owns the property.

PROPERTY HELD IN TRUST

BANK OR SECURITY ACCOUNT

If a bank account or security account is registered in the name of the decedent held "in trust for" or "for the benefit of" someone, then once the bank has a certified copy of the death certificate, the bank will turn over the account to the beneficiary. If the beneficiary is not yet 18, and the money in the account does not exceed $10,000, the bank may give the funds to the child's parent.

Permission from a Judge of the Probate Court will be needed to distribute monies in accounts that exceed $10,000. The Judge may require that a Custodian be appointed to care for the property until the child is an adult, or the Judge could decide to set up a guardianship to care for the child's property until the child reaches 18 (MGL 201A:6, 201:7).

BANK ACCOUNT HELD BY A TRUSTEE

If the bank or security account is registered in the name of the decedent "as Trustee under a Trust agreement," that means the decedent was the Trustee of a Trust and the bank will turn over that account to the Successor Trustee of the Trust. Banks usually require a copy of the Trust agreement when the account was opened, so the bank probably knows the identity of the Successor Trustee. If the Successor Trustee is deceased, and no other named, then the monies will go to the beneficiaries of Trust (MGL 167D:6).

REAL PROPERTY

If the decedent had a Trust and put property that he owned into the Trust, then the deed may read something like this:

> . . .
> JOHN ZAMORA and MARIA ZAMORA,
> of Worchester County, Massachusetts
> grants to
> JOHN ZAMORA, **trustee of the**
> **JOHN ZAMORA**
> **REVOCABLE TRUST AGREEMENT**
> DATED FEBRUARY 26, 2004,
> and his Successors, as Trustee,
> . . .

The death of the Trustee of a Trust does not change the ownership of the property. It remains in the Trust. The Trust document might say whether the person who takes John's place as Trustee (the Successor Trustee) should sell or keep the property or perhaps give it to a beneficiary. If no instruction is given, the Successor Trustee can use his discretion as to what to do with the property. His decision may be affected by laws relating to the administration of Trust property in the state where the property is located.

If you are a beneficiary of the Trust and you are concerned about what the Successor Trustee will do with the property, then it is best to consult with your attorney to learn about your rights under that Trust.

If the decedent owned property that was in his name only (not jointly or in trust for someone), then some sort of Probate procedure may be necessary before the heirs can get possession of that property. Chapter 6 explains how to get possession of the property.

Who is entitled to property held in the decedent's name only depends on whether the decedent died with or without a Will. If the decedent had a valid Will, the beneficiaries of the decedent's property are identified in the Will. If he died without a Will, the state of Massachusetts provides one for him in the form of its Laws of Descent and Distribution. These laws determine who is entitled to inherit his Probate Estate and what percentage of the Estate each heir is to receive once all the bills and costs of administering the Probate proceedings are paid (MGL 190:2). The law recognizes the right of the family to inherit the decedent's property. The law covers all possible relationships beginning with the decedent's spouse. But before we investigate the law, we need to know who the Commonwealth of Massachusetts considers to be the surviving spouse.

Who's The Spouse?
In this era of people challenging the concept of the family unit, those of a philosophical bent may ponder the meaning of marriage. Is it a union of two people in the eyes of God? Is it even a union? Maybe it is just a contract between two people. The state does not concern itself with such things. If the decedent was a resident of Massachusetts and died without a Will, his property is distributed according to the laws of the state; and the laws of the Commonwealth of Massachusetts determine whether the decedent was married.

BEING MARRIED IN MASSACHUSETTS

To be married in Massachusetts means that a man and a woman have obtained a license to marry from the state, solemnized the marriage by a state or religious ceremony, and then cohabited together as man and wife. The age of consent remains as it was under English Common Law, namely 12 for a female, 14 for a male, but people under the age of 18 cannot marry unless the marriage is authorized by a Probate or District Court (MGL 207:24, 207:25).

Massachusetts law prohibits the marriage of people:
- ☒ who are currently married;
- ☒ who are related closer than cousin;
- ☒ who are grandparent and grandchild;
- ☒ who are related through marriage as follows:

A man cannot marry his stepmother; stepdaughter; step-granddaughter, mother-in-law, grandmother-in-law, grandfather's former wife. He cannot marry his grandson's former wife, but there is no prohibition against marrying his son's former wife i.e. his daughter-in-law (MGL 207:1, 207:3, 207:4). There are similar prohibitions for a woman, with two exceptions — a woman cannot marry her former son-in-law, but she can marry her father-in-law (MGL 207:2).

THE COMMON LAW MARRIAGE

A common law marriage is one that has not been solemnized by ceremony. It is more than just living together. The couple must agree to live together as man and wife, and then publicly hold themselves out as being married. Although there is no specific law that bars a common law marriage, courts have ruled that such marriages are not valid in Massachusetts (*Commonwealth v. Munson*, 127 Mass 459). The surviving partner of such a union can inherit property as a beneficiary of the decedent's Will, but cannot inherit under the Massachusetts Laws of Descent and Distribution.

SAME SEX MARRIAGES

In 1999, the Massachusetts Supreme Judicial Court ruled that the City of Boston had the right to define the terms "domestic partners" and their "dependent" for the purpose of extending health benefit coverage. The opposition argued that this was tantamount to legalizing same sex marriages. None-the-less, the Court ruled in favor of the City of Boston (*Connors v. City of Boston*, 430 Mass. 31 (1999), 714 N.E.2d 335). In November, 2003, the Court took a more aggressive position and said that denying couples of the same sex the right to marry was a violation of their equal rights protection under the Massachusetts Constitution (*Goodridge v. Department of Public Health*, 440 Mass. 309 (2003)). That case was later upheld by the Massachusetts Supreme Judicial Court, so as of May 17, 2004, gay couples are free to marry within the state of Massachusetts.

THE DESERTED SPOUSE

A married person has the right to ask a Court to enter a judgment stating that the married person has been deserted by his/her spouse; or that the married person is living apart from his/her spouse for a justifiable cause. If the married person is incapacitated, then that person's guardian, or even a friend, can ask the Court for such a ruling. Once the Court makes the ruling, then should that married person die, the surviving spouse may not inherit property under the Massachusetts Laws of Descent and Distribution, nor is the surviving spouse entitled to any right of Dower (MGL 209:36).

As we have seen, in some cases, the question "Who's the spouse?" is not easily answered. It is important to consult with an attorney if you have any question about the right of a person to inherit as a surviving spouse.

If you die *intestate* (i.e., without a Will), your Probate Estate is distributed according to the Massachusetts *Laws of Descent and Distribution*. These laws are also referred to as the *Laws of Intestate Succession*.

SINGLE WITH DESCENDANTS
If you are single and are survived by *descendants* (children, grandchildren, great-grandchildren, etc.), your children inherit your Probate Estate in equal shares, *by right of representation* (MGL 190:1).

By right of representation is one of those legal terms that is best explained through example:

Suppose you are single and are survived by four children, Ann, Barry, Carl, David. If you do not have a valid Will, each of your children gets 25% of your Probate Estate. If Ann dies before you, leaving no descendants, your Probate Estate will be divided equally among your surviving children; namely Barry, Carl and David will each receive one third of your Probate Estate.

Suppose instead that only Carl and David survive you. If Ann died leaving one child and Barry died leaving 3 children, your Probate Estate is divided into 4 equal shares — one for each surviving child and one share for each deceased child who left descendants. Carl and David each get their 25% share. The share intended for Ann, namely 25% of your Probate Estate, is given to her child.

The share intended for Barry is divided between his three children. Each gets one third of the 25% or 8 1/3% of your Probate Estate.

MARRIED WITH DESCENDANTS

If you are married and have children, your spouse gets half of your Probate Estate and your children share the other half in equal shares, by right of representation.

NO SPOUSE, NO DESCENDANTS

If your have no surviving spouse and no surviving descendants, your Probate Estate goes to your parents equally or to the survivor of them. If neither parent survives you, your Probate Estate goes to your brothers and sisters, equally, by right of representation;

There is no distinction between full blood siblings or half blood siblings. For example, if you have one brother with the same set of parents, and another brother with the same father and a different mother, both brothers inherit an equal amount (MGL 190:4).

If you are not survived by a sibling, or any of their descendants (nephews, nieces, great nieces or nephews, etc.), then your Estate goes to your nearest next of kin (MGL 190:3).

SPOUSE, NO DESCENDANTS, BUT RELATIVES

If you have no descendants, but your are survived by a spouse and *kindred* (blood relatives) your spouse gets the first $200,000 of your Probate Estate and half of anything over that value. Your next of kin inherit the other half in the same manner as just described, i.e. your parents share the other half. If only one parent is alive, that parent gets the entire inheritance. If no parent survives you, then the half goes to your brothers and sisters, equally, by right of representation; etc.

THE COMMONWEALTH: HEIR OF LAST RESORT

In Massachusetts, property that is either unclaimed or abandoned, goes to the state, so if you die without a Will and you have absolutely no next of kin, or if you have a Will but no beneficiary can be found, then the Commonwealth of Massachusetts "inherits" your Probate Estate. The only exception is for a veteran who dies while a member of the Soldier's Home in Massachusetts. In that cases the inheritance goes to the legacy fund or legacy account of the Soldier's Home (MGL 190:3).

 IT ISN'T ALL THAT SIMPLE

The explanation in this book of the Massachusetts Laws of Descent and Distribution is abridged. We gave examples up to niece and nephew. Beyond that things get complicated. MGL190:3 reads:

> If he leaves no issue, and no father, mother, brother or sister and no issue of any deceased brother or sister, then to his next of kin in equal degree; but if there are two or more collateral kindred in equal degree claiming through different ancestors, those claiming through the nearest ancestor shall be preferred to those claiming through an ancestor more remote.

You might think you could puzzle this out if only you knew what a "degree" means. The next section 190:4 reads:

> Degrees of kindred shall be computed according to the rules of the civil law.

Now you are probably thinking "Well I guess lawyers understand all this." But to a lawyer it just means that if someone dies without a Will and several distant heirs all make claim to the property, he is going to spend a lot of time doing research in the law library.

WHO DIED FIRST?

Sometimes it happens that two family members die simultaneously, and no one knows who died first. For example, suppose a husband and wife die together in an car crash, how is their property distributed?

Massachusetts statute provides for an orderly distribution of the respective Estates in such cases. Each person is assumed to have survived the other and the property of each is distributed on that basis. The husband's property is distributed as if he survived his wife and the wife's property is distributed as if she survived her husband. For example, suppose the husband is insured, with his wife as beneficiary. The proceeds of the policy will be distributed as if the wife died before her husband. The proceeds will be given to the alternate beneficiary named in the policy. If no alternate beneficiary was named, the proceeds of the policy will go to the insured party (in this case, the husband).

Property owned jointly by the couple, with no provision for who is to inherit the property should they both die, is divided with half going to the Estate of the husband and the other half to the Estate of the wife. If they each have a Will, the husband's half is distributed according to his Will and the wife's half according to her Will. If they die without a Will, then the husband's half is distributed according to the Massachusetts Laws of Descent and Distribution as if he were single; and vis-versa (MGL 190A:3, 190A:4, 191:1A).

THE RIGHTS OF A CHILD

ADOPTED CHILD

An adopted child has the same rights to inherit property under the Laws of Descent from his adoptive parents as does a natural child. Whether the adoptive child can inherit from his natural parents depends on the circumstances of the adoption. If one of the child's parents dies, and the child is later adopted by a stepparent, then that child still retains full rights of inheritance from both of his natural parents, and their respective families. But if a Court terminates the rights of his natural parent(s), then that includes the right to inherit property from his natural parents and from his natural relatives (MGL 210:7, 210:8).

NON-MARITAL CHILD

A child born out of wedlock has the right to inherit from his/her father and the father's relatives, provided

☑ the father acknowledged the child as his own - or -

☑ paternity was established by a Court of law in this or any other state (MGL 190:7).

If the decedent denied his paternity, then it will take a Court procedure to establish (or disprove) paternity.   If you want to establish paternity, then you need to consult with an attorney who is experienced in this type of litigation. If DNA tests need to be conducted, and the family plans to cremate the decedent, you may need to have your attorney move quickly to bar cremation until the matter is settled.

NO SHARE FOR NEGLECTFUL FATHER

If a child born out of wedlock dies, and his father did not treat the child as his own or was not determined to be the child's father by a Court, then neither the father nor his family members can inherit anything from the child (MGL 190:6).

Medical technology has made important contributions to solving the problem of infertility. There are all sorts of solutions, from hormone replacement therapy, to sperm banks that provide donations anonymously, to frozen sperm and/or ova to be thawed and used at a later date, to a woman who agrees to be a surrogate or gestation mother, for an intended genetic parent. Solving a set of medical problems has opened the door to a new set of legal problems. Used to be, the only question was "Who's the father?" Now it could well be "Who's the mother? We will examine Massachusetts law as it relates to the right of a child born of an assisted conception to inherit property.

In general, a child born to parents using any form of assisted conception, has the same right to inherit from his parents as a child conceived the old fashioned way. A child conceived by means of artificial insemination born to a married woman with the consent of her husband is the legal child of both parents (MGL 46:4B). If the husband did not know or consent to such assisted conception, he can petition the Court to terminate his parental rights and responsibilities. If the husband is successful the child will not be able to inherit from the husband, nor his family.

FROZEN SPERM AND THE AFTERBORN CHILD
Under Massachusetts law a child conceived prior to death and born after the parent died has the same right to inherit as those alive at birth (MGL 190:8). But what if the child was conceived after death? That question was answered by the Massachusetts Supreme Court. The case involved twins born to a woman two years after her husband died from leukemia. He had his sperm frozen before starting his cancer treatment. The treatment was not successful and he died within the year. His wife used the sperm to conceive the twins after his death.

She applied for Social Security benefits for herself and children. The U.S. District Court rejected the claim saying that the children did not qualify for benefits because they could not inherit under Massachusetts Laws of Descent. She appealed, and the District Court asked the Massachusetts Supreme Judicial Court to settle the issue. The Supreme Judicial Court ruled that a child conceived and born after the death of a parent can inherit, provided it is proven that the decedent is the genetic parent and had consented to posthumous conception and to the support of any resulting child (*Woodward v. Commr. of Social Security*, SJC-0840 (Mass. January 2, 2002)).

THE SURROGATE PARENT

A case brought before the Supreme Judicial Court asked whether an agreement for adoption between a surrogate mother and the genetic father of her child was legally enforceable. The surrogate mother changed her mind after the birth and the genetic father sued for adoption of the child. The Court found that the agreement between the surrogate parents and genetic father was not enforceable because the agreement for adoption was made before the child was born. Under Massachusetts law (MGL 210:2), no adoption agreement is valid unless the agreement was made on or after the fourth day following the child's birth (*R.R. v. M.H.*, 426 Mass. 501 (1998), 689 N.E.2d 790).

Under current Massachusetts law, the child of the surrogate mother, is the mother of the child. If she is married and her husband agreed to the procedure, then he is the legal father of the child (MGL 46:4B). After birth the surrogate parents can agree to the adoption of the child by the intended (genetic) parents. Adoption is necessary, regardless of whether either (or both) of the intended parents happen to be the genetic parent of the child.

WHEN TO CHALLENGE THE WILL

It is not uncommon for a family member to be unhappy with the way the decedent willed his property. If you are tempted to challenge a Will, first consider whether the Will is valid. In Massachusetts, a Will is presumed to be valid if at the time he signed the Will the decedent was at least 18 and of sound mind (MGL 191:1). Massachusetts courts have ruled that a Will maker is considered to be of sound mind if:

☑ he knew what property he had; and,

☑ he understood his relation to those people who would naturally have expected to be remembered; and

☑ he was not suffering from a mental disorder affecting his ability to distribute his property; and

☑ he knew what he was doing (namely making a Will); (*Palmer v. Palmer*, 23 Mass. App. Ct. 245 (1986), 500 N.E.2d 1354).

Even if the decedent was of sound mind, a Will can be challenged on by showing that the Will maker was pressured into preparing his Will a certain way; i.e., that someone used *undue influence* and that the decedent was not acting voluntarily or intelligently, but rather according to the will of someone who dominated him.

If you can prove the decedent was under 18 when he signed the Will, you have it made. Challenging the Will on other grounds may be difficult — especially if the Will was prepared by the decedent's attorney, who will, no doubt, testify that the Will maker's mind was perfectly clear when he signed the document; and that he signed it of his own free will. But difficult is not impossible. If you are concerned about the validity of the Will, it is important to consult with an attorney experienced in Probate litigation.

THE UNWITNESSED WILL

Massachusetts statute requires that a Will be in writing and signed by the person who is making the Will in the presence of two or more competent witnesses. A beneficiary of the Will can be a witness to the Will, but the gift to the beneficiary, or to his/her spouse, will not be given to the beneficiary (or his/her spouse) unless there are two other witnesses to the Will.

The first step in the Probate procedure is to have the Probate Court determine whether the Will presented is valid. If the Will is in writing and signed by the Will maker in the presence of at least two independent witnesses, then there should be no problem in having the Will accepted into Probate. If the Will is notarized, then the Court will probably not require any witnesses to testify. If the Will is witnessed but not notarized, then the Court will ask that at least one of the witnesses testify that they saw the Will maker sign the Will (MGL 191:2).

But suppose the decedent wrote out a Will in his own hand and signed it with no one present? Such a Will is called a *holographic Will*. Many states, including Massachusetts, refuse to accept a holographic Will into Probate. The problem with a holographic Will, in this or any other state, is its authenticity. Because no one saw the decedent sign the Will, it is hard to determine whether the Will was written by the decedent or is a forgery.

If all that the decedent left was an unwitnessed, handwritten Will, the Probate Court will not admit the document into Probate and the decedent's property will be distributed according to the Massachusetts Laws of Descent and Distribution (MGL 191:7).

THE VERBAL WILL

Picture a death bed scene. The elderly gentleman is surrounded by several family members. In a whisper, just audible enough to be heard, he says:

"Even though I am a wealthy man, I never got around to making a Will. You all have been good to me, but I wanted my entire fortune to go to my nephew, Robert. He has been like a son to me. "

Do you think Robert can inherit his Uncle's Estate?

Not in Massachusetts unless:
⇨ Someone writes down his uncles's wishes, and
⇨ The uncle acknowledges that this is his Will, and
⇨ The uncle tells someone to sign the Will for him, and
⇨ The person does so, and two people sign the Will as witnesses (MGL 191:1).

Considering that the uncle's relatives will probably inherit the fortune under Massachusetts's Laws of Descent and Distribution, it is doubtful that Robert is in danger of becoming wealthy at any time in the near future.

EXCEPTION FOR SOLDIERS AND MARINERS
There is an exception to the rule that the Will must be in writing and that is the case of a soldier in actual military service or a mariner at sea. The soldier (or mariner) can explain who is to inherit his property. Should the soldier or mariner then die, the testimony of the witness will be sufficient for the Probate Court to distribute the property according to the last wishes of the soldier or mariner (MGL 191:6).

THE WILL THAT IS CONTRARY TO LAW

Sometimes a person who is of sound mind, makes a Will, but that Will has the effect of giving a spouse or a minor child less than is required under Massachusetts law. One such example is that of Nancy. Hers was not an easy life. She worked long hours as a waitress. She divorced her hard-drinking first husband. The final judgment gave her their home, some cash and securities, and sole custody of their son, Richard. After the divorce Nancy had her attorney prepare a Will leaving all she owned to her son. Some years later she met and married Harry, a chef at the restaurant where she worked. He moved into her home and they later had a daughter. Richard was 19, and his stepsister 12, when Nancy died after a lengthy battle with cancer.

Nancy did not leave much — a savings account of $50,000, a car, and her home, all of which was in her name only. Before she died, she told Richard, that she had not changed her Will because she wanted him to have all she owned. She said Harry had a good job and she was sure he would take good care of his daughter.

No sooner was the funeral over, when Nancy's son came in and demanded that Harry vacate his mother's home. Harry was furious and went to his attorney.

"I was a good husband to Nancy, supporting and caring for her during her illness. It was me, and not her son, who was at her side when she died. Don't I have any rights? And what about my daughter. Doesn't she have any rights?"

The attorney explained "Under Massachusetts law, every parent must make some provision for his child in his Will. A child who is not mentioned in the Will has the right to inherit as much as she would have inherited if the parent died intestate (without a Will), unless it appears from the Will that the omission was intentional, or unless the parent made other provision for the child. In fact, in Massachusetts, a parent must make provision in his/her Will for the child of their deceased child; otherwise, the parent's grandchild has the same rights as did the child of the parent. In this case, your daughter is entitled to 25% of her mother's Estate" (MGL 191:20, 191:25).

The attorney continued "If your wife filed a Declaration of Homestead, then your daughter has the right to occupy the homestead until she reaches the age of 18, and you can continue to live there until you remarry or die (MGL 188:2, 188:4)."

"No, I don't believe that she ever did."

"You still have many rights under Massachusetts law, provided you did not give up those rights (MGL 209:25). Did you sign a prenuptial or postnuptial Agreement giving up any of your rights?"

"Absolutely not!"

"In that case, you have the right to keep all of your wife's clothing and jewelry. You have the right to live in your wife's house rent free for up to six months. You can ask the Judge of the Probate Court to allow you to keep as much of the furnishings as you may need for you and your daughter. And unless your wife gave her car as a gift in her Will, you have the right to transfer the car to your name." (MGL 90D:15A, 196:1, 196:2).

Harry wondered "Don't I have Curtesy rights?"

The attorney explained "In Massachusetts, Curtesy rights are the same as the wife's Dower rights. You have the right to take the amount provided for you in the Will (in this case nothing) or you can take a one-third Life Estate in all of the real property owned by your wife at the time of her death." (MGL 189:1).

"How do I occupy one-third of our house, if Richard owns the other two-thirds?"

The attorney said "There are several ways to solve the problem. You could have the Court determine the fair market rental value of the property. Let's say the rental value is $900. Your Dower interest is worth one-third of the $900 ($300). You would need to pay Richard the balance of the rent, that is $600 a month."

"I don't think that arrangement will work out."

The attorney offered an alternative "The house could be sold. Your Dower interest can be evaluated by the Probate Court and you would receive as much of the proceeds to compensate you for your Dower interest. Or your could use the Court valuation to buy out Richard's share of the property and continue to live there."

Harry was not pleased "You mean that all I am entitled to is this one-third Life Estate in the home?"

The attorney said "Instead of your Dower right you could take an *Elective Share* of all of your wife's property. In Massachusetts, the Elective Share depends on the value of the Estate, and whether the decedent left descendants or blood relatives. In your case, she left descendants, so you are entitled to one-third of all her real and personal property, but if that share is worth more than $25,000, you can take $25,000 outright and the income for life from the remaining one-third share (MGL 191:15, 191:17).

"I'll do better to take the Elective share instead of the Dower, so I'll take the car, the house furnishings; six months free rent and my Elective Share."

"Not so fast. You will need file your election with the Registry of Probate within 6 months of your wife's death; and the Court will need to rule on these matters."

Harry did get the car, the furnishings, the 6 months free rent, and his Elective Share. Nancy's daughter inherited one quarter of the Estate and the rest went to Richard. Richard did not fare as well as his mother planned. There was no cash left in the Estate after paying the funeral expenses, medical bills, and the costs of probating the Estate, and Harry's $25,000. All Richard inherited was his fractional share of the house. And he didn't get that until the house was sold a year later.

No doubt Nancy did not understand what would happen to her Estate when she passed on. If she knew about the law, she could have consulted with an attorney and set up an Estate plan that would have come closer to achieving her goal of providing for Richard. More importantly, had she included Harry in the plan, there might not have been the turmoil and hard feelings that were a result of the Will she did leave.

But, the moral of the story, for the purpose of this discussion, is that if you believe that the decedent's Will is not valid or is not drafted according to Massachusetts law, then you need to consult with an attorney experienced in Probate matters to determine your legal rights under the Will.

Getting Possession Of The Property 6

Knowing who is entitled to receive the decedent's property is one thing. Getting that property is another. As explained in the previous chapter if the decedent held property jointly with someone, or in a Trust for someone, the property now belongs to the joint owner or beneficiary. If it is personal property such as a bank account or a security, the beneficiary can usually get possession of the property by giving a certified copy of the death certificate to the financial institution.

If the decedent held real or personal property in his name only, or as a Tenant In Common, then some sort of Probate procedure may be required in order to transfer ownership to the proper beneficiary. If a full Probate procedure is necessary, then you will need the assistance of an attorney. But there are a few items that can be transferred without legal assistance. This chapter explains how to get possession of such items.

This chapter also contains an explanation of the different kinds of Probate procedure and when it is appropriate to use that procedure.

DISTRIBUTING PERSONAL EFFECTS

Too often, the first person to discover the body will help himself to the decedent's *personal effects* (clothing, jewelry, appliances, electrical equipment, cameras, books, household items and furnishing, etc.). Unless that person is the decedent's sole beneficiary, such action is unconscionable, if not illegal.

If the decedent was married, then the decedent's clothing and personal jewelry belong to his spouse unless he left a Will giving a particular item of personal property to someone else. If the decedent was not married but had minor child(ren), then his clothing and jewelry go to the child(ren). The spouse or minor child(ren) also have the right to ask the Court to allow them to keep as much of the decedent's personal property as is necessary for their everyday living (see Chapter 4) (MGL 196:1, 196:2).

If the decedent was not married, then all of his personal effects should be given to the person appointed as the Personal Representative. The Representative then has the duty to distribute the property according to the decedent's Will, or if no Will, then according to the Laws of Descent and Distribution.

If you determine that there is no need for a Probate procedure and the decedent did not have a Will, then his next of kin need to divide all of the personal effects among themselves in approximately equal proportions. Most personal effects have little, if any, monetary value. Furniture may be worth less than it costs to ship. In such case, the beneficiaries may decide to donate the personal property to the decedent's favorite charity.

What's Equal?

The decedent's Will may direct that the decedent's personal property be divided equally between two or more beneficiaries. The problem with the term "equal" is that people have different ideas of what "equal" means. Unless there is clear evidence that the decedent's Will meant something else, "equal" refers to the monetary value of the item and not to the number of items received. For example, to divide the decedent's personal effects equally, one beneficiary may receive an expensive item of jewelry and another beneficiary may receive several items whose overall value is approximately equal to that single piece of jewelry.

When distributing personal effects there needs to be cooperation and perhaps compromise, or else bitter arguments might arise over items of little monetary value.

One such argument occurred when an elderly woman died who was rich only in her love for her five children and nine grandchildren. After the funeral, the children gathered in their mother's apartment. Each child had his own furnishings and no need for anything in the apartment. They agreed to donate all of their mother's personal effects to a local charity with the exception of a few items of sentimental value.

Each child took some small item as a remembrance — a handkerchief, a large platter that their mother used to serve family dinners, a doily their mother crocheted. Things went smoothly until it came to her photograph album. Frank, the youngest sibling, said, "I'll take this." Marie objected saying, "But there are pictures in that album that I want."

Frank retorted, "You already took all the pictures Mom had on her dresser."

The argument went downhill from there. Unsettled sibling rivalries boiled over, fueled by the hurt of the loss that they were all experiencing.

It almost came to blows when the eldest settled the argument: "Frank you make copies of all of the photos in the album for Marie. Marie, you make copies of all of the pictures that you took and give them to Frank. This way you both will have a complete set of Mom's pictures. And while you're at it, make copies for the rest of us."

NON-PROBATE TRANSFERS

A **Non-probate transfer** is a transfer of the decedent's property without the need for Probate. For example, if the decedent had a bank account that he owned jointly with another. The surviving joint owner can withdraw the funds from the bank. If the decedent owned a bank account in his name only "in trust for" someone or with instructions to "pay on death" to a someone, all the beneficiary need do is produce a death certificate and proper identification, and the bank will turn over the property to the beneficiary.

Securities that are held jointly with someone, or with instructions to "transfer on death" to a named beneficiary, can be transferred to that beneficiary in the same manner.

Later in this chapter, we will discuss the Non-probate transfer of real property.

TRANSFERRING THE CAR

If the decedent owned a motor vehicle in his name only, then title to the car needs to be transferred to the new owner and new owner needs to register the car in the state where it will be driven. You may want to limit the use of the car until it is transferred to the beneficiary. If the decedent's car is involved in an accident before the car is transferred to the new owner, then the decedent's Estate may be liable for the damage. Having adequate insurance on the car may save the Estate from monetary loss, but a pending lawsuit could delay Probate and prevent any money from being distributed to the beneficiaries until the lawsuit is settled.

If there is a Probate procedure then it is the Personal Representative's job to transfer the motor vehicles to the proper beneficiary. If the decedent had a Will and he made a specific gift of the car to someone, then the Personal Representative will transfer the car to that person. If no mention was made in the Will, it goes to the surviving spouse. And if there is no surviving spouse, the car goes to the *residuary beneficiaries* under the Will, i.e., those who inherit whatever is left once all the bills have been paid and all the special gifts made in the Will are distributed.

If the decedent died without a Will, then the car goes to the surviving spouse; and if there is no surviving spouse, then to the decedent's heirs as determined by the Laws of Descent and Distribution (MGL 90D:15A).

TRANSFER WHEN MORE THAN ONE BENEFICIARY

If there is more than one person who has the right to inherit the car, then they all can take title to the car. That may not be a practical thing to do since only one person can drive the car at any given time and if one gets into an accident, they all can be held liable. The better route is for the beneficiaries to agree to have one person take title to the car. The person taking title will need to compensate the others for their share of the car. In such case, the beneficiaries need to come to an agreement as to the value of the car.

DETERMINING THE VALUE OF THE CAR

Cars are valued in different ways. The *collateral* value of the car is the value that banks use to evaluate the car for purposes of making a loan to the owner. If you were to trade in a car for the purpose of purchasing a new one, the car dealer would offer you its *wholesale* value. Were you to purchase that same car from a car dealer, he would price it at its *retail* or *fair market value*. Usually the retail price is highest, wholesale is lowest and the collateral value of the car is somewhere in between.

You can call your local bank to get the collateral value of the car. It may be more difficult to obtain the wholesale value of the car because the amount of money a dealer is willing to pay for the car depends on the value of the new car that you are purchasing. You can determine the car's retail value by looking at comparable used car advertisements in the local newspaper. Rather than going through the effort of determining these three values, you can use your Internet search engine to look up the Kelly Blue Book Value. This publication gives Low, Average and High Blue Book Values which correspond to the wholesale, collateral and retail values.

MAKING THE TRANSFER

No Probate procedure is necessary to transfer the car to the surviving spouse. The spouse can go to the nearest Registry of Motor Vehicles and they will assist with the transfer. They will require a certified copy of the death certificate. It is a good idea to first call the local Registry to determine the current transfer fee and whether there is any other document they may require.

Transferring the car to anyone else requires authorization from the Probate Court. If the car is the only item that is in the decedent's name only and its value is not greater than $15,000, you can use the Informal Administration procedure as explained later in this chapter. A full Probate procedure is necessary for values greater than $15,000.

Once you have authorization, you can go to the Registry of Motor Vehicles and make the transfer. You will probably want to transfer the car registration at the same time you change title to the car. If the car is going to be transferred out of state, then the Massachusetts registration needs to be cancelled.

You can get information about what documents and information is necessary to make the transfer by calling the Registry of Motor Vehicles at (617) 351-4500. You can find information and the name and address of your nearest Registry of Motor Vehicles on the Internet.

 THE REGISTRY OF MOTOR VEHICLES
http://www.state.ma.us/rmv

CANCELING THE DRIVER'S LICENSE

It is important to notify the Registry of Motor Vehicles of the death and to turn in the decedent's driver's license or photo identification card record. The Department will take the decedent off of their mailing list. This will assist the Department in preventing others from using the decedent's name for fraudulent purposes.

TRANSFERRING THE MOBILE HOME

A mobile home is a motor vehicle, so the method just described can be used to transfer title to the decedent's mobile home. Before making the transfer, you need to find out whether the land on which the mobile home is located was leased or owned by the decedent. If the decedent was renting space in a trailer park, then you need to contact the trailer park owner to transfer the lease agreement to the beneficiary of the mobile home.

If the decedent owned the land under the mobile home, then a Probate procedure will be necessary to transfer the land to the proper beneficiary. We will discuss how to transfer real property, later in this Chapter.

The leased car is not an asset of the Estate because the decedent did not own the car. The leased car is a liability to the Estate because the decedent was obligated to pay the balance of the monies owed on the lease agreement. The Personal Representative, or next of kin, needs to work out an agreement with the company to either assign the lease to a beneficiary or family member who will agree to pay for the lease — or to have the Estate pay off the lease by purchasing the car under the terms of the lease agreement.

Some lenders will allow the lease to be assigned to a beneficiary provided the Estate remains liable for the balance of payment. In such cases, it is better to have the beneficiary refinance the car and have the original lease agreement paid in full.

If the remaining payments exceed the current market value of the car, there may be a temptation to hand the keys over to the leasing company. This may not be the best strategy, because the leasing company can sell the car and then sue the Estate for the balance of the monies owed. If the decedent had no assets or if the only assets he had are creditor proof, then simply returning the car may be an option. But if the decedent's Estate has assets available to pay the balance of the lease payments, then the Personal Representative needs to arrange to have the car transferred in a way that releases the Estate from all further liability.

TRANSFERRING THE MOTORBOAT

In Massachusetts, motorboats 14' or longer, must be titled and registered with the Registration and Titling Section of the Massachusetts Department of Fisheries, Wildlife and Environmental Law Enforcement ("DFWELE"). The beneficiary of the decedent's motorboat must obtain a new title and registration within 30 days of inheriting the decedent's motorboat (MGL 90B:36). You can get information about transferring the title and registration by calling (617) 626-1610) or you can download registration forms from the DFWELE Web site.

 DFWELE LICENSING AND REGISTRATION
http://www.state.ma.us/dfwele

TRANSFERRING AIRCRAFT

The Massachusetts Aeronautics Commission is in charge of the registration of aircraft that is based in, or primarily used within, the state (MGL 90:49). If the decedent owned an aircraft, the Personal Representative will need to arrange to transfer title to the proper beneficiary by contacting the Aircraft Registration Branch of the Federal Aviation Administration (405) 954-3116.

The new owner will need to arrange for his own state registration. He can call the Commission at (617) 973-8881, or he can get information about the registration of aircraft by visiting their Web site.

 THE MASSACHUSETTS AERONAUTICS COMMISSION
http://www.massaeronautics.org

THE FEDERAL INCOME TAX REFUND

Any refund due to the decedent under a joint federal income tax return filed by his surviving spouse will be sent to the surviving spouse. If the decedent's Personal Representative filed the final return, then the refund check will be sent to him to be deposited to the Estate account.

If the decedent was single and no Probate proceeding is necessary, then whoever is entitled to the decedent's Estate is entitled to the refund check. If you are the beneficiary of the decedent's Estate, you can obtain the refund by filing IRS form 1310 along with the decedent's final income tax return (the 1040). You can obtain form 1310 from the decedent's accountant, or if he did not have an accountant and you wish to file yourself, you can call the IRS at (800) 829-3676 to obtain the form.

You can download instructions, publications and forms from the Internal Revenue Service by going to the **FORMS AND PUBLICATIONS** section of their Web site.

INTERNAL REVENUE SERVICE
http://www.irs.gov/

The Personal Representative does not need to file form 1310 because once he files the decedent's final income tax return, any refund will be forwarded to him. Similarly, it is not necessary for the surviving spouse who filed a joint return to file form 1310.

THE STATE INCOME TAX REFUND

The decedent's final Massachusetts State income tax return needs to be filed at the same time the federal income tax return is filed. The surviving spouse can file a joint return. Any refund will be sent to the surviving spouse. If the decedent was not married and a Probate procedure is necessary, then the Personal Representative will file the final return. Any refund will be given to him to be deposited to the Estate account.

If no Probate procedure is necessary, and the decedent was not married, then the next of kin can file the return. If you need information about filing the final return, you can call in state (800) 392-6089. Out of state, call (617) 887-6367. You can also get information from the Massachusetts Department of Revenue Web site.

 MASSACHUSETTS DEPARTMENT OF REVENUE
http://www.state.ma.us/dor

DEPOSITING THE TAX REFUND
If the refund check is sent to the Personal Representative, then he will deposit it to the Estate account. If there is no Probate procedure and the refund check (or any other check) is in the name of the decedent, you can deposit it into the decedent's bank account. You can obtain all of the money in that account by using the appropriate Probate procedure. If the account contains less than $10,000, you may be able to get the money without going through any Probate administration. See the next page for an explanation of how to obtain the money in the account.

NO ADMINISTRATION NECESSARY

There are certain items that can be transferred to certain beneficiaries without the need for Probate. As discussed, a motor vehicle that was in the decedent's name only, or held jointly with his spouse, can be transferred to the surviving spouse without the need for Probate administration. Other items that can bypass Probate are:

✧ WAGES UP TO $100 ✧

The decedent's employer can give the final paycheck to the surviving spouse, or an adult child, or if none of these, to the decedent's parent, provided:

⇨ the wages do not exceed $100, and

⇨ the decedent died without a Will, and

⇨ at least 30 days passed since the date of death, and

⇨ no one started a Probate procedure (MGL 149:178A).

This law applies only to employees in the private sector. It does not apply if the decedent was employed by the Commonwealth of Massachusetts.

✧ INSURANCE PROCEEDS TO ESTATE UP TO $10,000 ✧

A health insurance company that owes money to the decedent can pay those funds to the surviving spouse, or if no spouse, then to his next of kin, provided:

⇨ the proceeds do not exceed $10,000, and

⇨ the decedent was a resident of Massachusetts, and

⇨ at least 60 days passed since the date of death, and

⇨ no written claim from a Personal Representative has been received at the company's home office.

This also applies to other types of insurance policies such as life or accident insurance, annuities or endowment policies. Specifically, if all of the above criteria are met, insurance proceeds payable to the decedent's Estate can be paid to the spouse or next of kin (MGL 175:187E).

✧ SECURITIES UP TO $2,100 ✧

Up to $2,100 in stocks can be transferred to the surviving spouse, or if no spouse, to an adult child, or if no child, then the mother or father of the decedent, provided:

⇨ only $750 be transferred by any one issuer; and

⇨ the total amount of securities transferred does not exceed $2,100; and

⇨ at least 30 days passed since the date of death, and

⇨ no written claim from a Personal Representative has been received (MGL 196:9).

✧ BANK DEPOSITS UP TO $10,000 ✧

A bank officer can give money held in an account in the decedent's name only, to the surviving spouse, or if no spouse, to the next of kin, provided:

⇨ the amount on deposit is no more than $10,000, and

⇨ at least 30 days passed since the date of death, and

⇨ no written claim from a Personal Representative has been received at the company's home office, and

⇨ the bank is given the deposit book (or other document evidencing the deposit) and a copy of the death certificate (MGL 167D:33).

These rules also apply to monies held in a credit union account, except the transfer cannot be made until 60 days have passed and the transfer cannot exceed $3,000 (MGL 171:42).

Neither the bank nor the securities company is required to permit the transfer. The company may decide to give the funds to the Personal Representative, or to someone given authority by the Probate Court. In such case, you will need to go through a Probate procedure. If the decedent's Probate Estate is no more than $15,000, you can use the Informal Administration procedure that is described on the next page.

INFORMAL ADMINISTRATION

The decedent's personal property can be transferred to someone who volunteers to informally administer the Estate; i.e., collect the assets, pay the bills, and then distribute whatever remains to the proper beneficiary. *Informal Administration* is allowed provided:

⇨ the Probate Estate consists of personal property worth no more than $15,000; and

⇨ the decedent was a resident of Massachusetts, and

⇨ at least 30 days passed since the date of death, and

⇨ no one started a Probate procedure.

WHO CAN VOLUNTEER

Massachusetts law requires that a *Voluntary Personal Representative* be an adult resident of the Commonwealth. Whoever volunteers must do so without any pay for his efforts. The person named as Executor of the decedent's Will can volunteer, but if he cannot or will not agree to serve voluntarily, then any of the following family members can volunteer: spouse, child, parent, brother, sister, niece, nephew, aunt, uncle. If none of these agree to serve, then a Full Probate procedure may be necessary. (MGL 195:16, 195.16A).

Whoever volunteers will need to go to the Probate Court in the county of the decedent's residence. You can look up their number in the telephone book or on the Internet. The National Center For State Courts has a Web site where you can find the address, phone number, office hours for local Court houses.

 NATIONAL CENTER FOR STATE COURTS
http://www.ncsc.dni.us/

THE INFORMAL ADMINISTRATION PROCEDURE

If you are the volunteer, then you will need to complete a form that you will receive from the Register of the Probate Court. To complete the form you will need the following information:

➡ the names and addresses of people who inherit the property according to the decedent's Will, or if no Will, then those who are entitled to inherit the property under the Massachusetts Laws of Descent and Distribution.

➡ a description of the items that need to be transferred and the value of each item.

➡ the names and addresses of the surviving joint owners of property held by the decedent and the joint owner.

You will need to give the Register of Probate a certified copy of the death certificate and pay a filing fee (currently $30) (MGL 262:40).

You might save time if you first call the Register. Some questions you may want answered:

What is the best time to meet with you?
What documents do I need to bring with me?
What is the current fee for Informal Administration?

NOTICE TO CREDITORS

The Voluntary Personal Representative must send, by certified mail, a copy of the completed Probate Court form and a certified copy of the death certificate to the Division of Medical Assistance (MGL 118E:32). The Register will give you the mailing address. If the decedent was receiving medical assistance, the Division Of Medical Assistance has four months from the date you file the Informal Administration form with the Register, to file a claim.

MAKING THE TRANSFER

The Register of Probate will give you documents that authorize you to take possession of the decedent's property. If you are trying to trying to get possession of a security, you will present the document to the company that issued the stock or bond. If you are trying to transfer the decedent's motor vehicle, you can present the document to the Registry of Motor Vehicles.

Once you have possession of the decedent's property, you may need to convert it to cash and use the money to pay for outstanding funeral expenses, costs of his last illness. You can use the funds to reimburse yourself for costs associated with the Voluntary Administration (filing fees, sending certified mail, etc.), but as mentioned, you cannot pay yourself for serving as Voluntary Representative. If there are any outstanding debts, then they need to be paid in the order given on page 97 of this book. You will distribute any funds remaining after bills are paid to the proper beneficiary. It is important that you do not distribute to a beneficiary unless you are sure that all debts are paid. If a creditor appears after you distributed the funds, then you may find yourself personally liable for that debt.

 MORE DEBTS THAN MONEY

It is important to check out all debts before you decide to become a Volunteer Representative. If you find that there are more debts than funds in the Estate, then you could be risking personal liability. Even if you do everything according to law, some of the creditors may challenge your decisions and demand that you pay the bill. Best to consult with an attorney before volunteering yourself into a bad situation.

TRANSFERRING REAL PROPERTY

If the decedent owned real property in his name only, or if the decedent owned property as a Tenant in Common, then some sort of Probate procedure will be necessary in order to transfer the parcel to the proper beneficiary.

No Probate procedure is necessary to transfer real property if the decedent held that property:
⇨   as the owner of a Life Estate   — or —
⇨   as a Joint Tenant   — or —
⇨   as Tenants By The Entirety

If you are the surviving joint owner and you wish to sell or transfer the property, you will need to give a certified copy of the death certificate to the attorney who does the closing, to prove that you are the sole owner. If you do not intend to sell or transfer the property in the near future, you may want to have your attorney prepare and record a document called a Deceased Joint Tenancy Affidavit. The Deceased Joint Tenancy Affidavit identifies the property, giving the property address, the Permanent Real Estate Index Number, and the full legal description of the property. A certified copy of the death certificate is attached to the Affidavit.

Once the Affidavit is recorded with the Register of Deeds in the county where the property is located, anyone who examines the title to the property will know that one of the joint owners died and that surviving joint tenants now own the property.

 **LAWYER**

TRANSFERRING OUT OF STATE PROPERTY

Each state regulates the transfer of real property within that state. Several states have rules much like Massachusetts, namely, an Affidavit is recorded that notifies anyone who is examining title to the property describing the transfer of title to the surviving joint owner or to the remainder beneficiary of a Life Estate interest.

A few states, such as Florida, allow the death certificate to be recorded in the county where the property is located, so that anyone who examines title to the property will know that the owner is deceased. In Florida, the Clerk of the Circuit Court is in charge of recording deeds and death certificates. In other states, it may be the County Registrar or the County Recorder.

It is the practice in other states not to record any document at all. In such states, the surviving owner needs to keep a certified copy of the death certificate to produce at closing should he later decide to sell or transfer the property.

If the decedent owned out of state real property Jointly With Rights of Survivorship, or if he held a Life Estate interest, you may want to contact the person in charge of recording deeds, or an attorney, to determine what documents need to be recorded at this time. And of course, if the decedent owned real property in his own name or as a Tenant In Common, you need to contact an attorney experienced in Probate matters to have the property transferred to the proper beneficiary.

If the decedent left real property in his name only or if the decedent left personal property worth more than $15,000, then there needs to be a full Probate Administration. The procedure can take anywhere from several months to more than a year depending on the size and complexity of the Probate Estate. It is the Personal Representative's job to use the Probate Estate to pay all valid claims and then to distribute what is left to the proper beneficiary.

All of the decedent's debts are paid from the Probate Estate and not from Personal Representative's pocket; but if the Personal Representative makes a mistake then he may be responsible to pay for that mistake (MGL 195:17). For example, suppose the Personal Representative pays a debt that did not need to be paid, or perhaps he transfers property to the beneficiaries too quickly and there were still taxes due on the Estate. In such cases the Personal Representative may be responsible to pay for such error.

The Personal Representative needs to employ an attorney to guide him through the process. It then becomes the job of the attorney for the Personal Representative to see to it that the Estate is administered properly and without any personal liability to the Representative. The attorney has the right to receive reasonable fees for his services and those fees are a proper charge to the decedent's Estate.

THE TEMPORARY PERSONAL REPRESENTATIVE

Sometimes it happens that there is some problem, either with accepting the Will into Probate, or perhaps a disagreement as to who should serve as Personal Representative. Rather than postpone the Probate procedure, the heirs may decide to have a *Temporary Representative* appointed. The Temporary Representative has much the same powers as a Personal Representative. He can collect the Estate property. He can, with Court authority, sell real estate, continue the decedent's business, pay certain claims, and pay an allowance to the spouse or minor child for their necessary living expenses. Other than the spouse's allowance, he cannot distribute property to the beneficiaries (MGL 192:13, 192:14, 193:7A).

The Temporary Representative is authorized to act for 90 days or until a Personal Representative is authorized to act, whichever is earlier. The Temporary Representative must, within 30 days of his discharge, turn over all of the Estate property to the Personal Representative and give a full accounting of actions taken (MGL 205:1).

Appointing a Temporary Representative, tends to increase the cost of Probate. Unless the Temporary Representative later serves as Personal Representative, there will be a cost of transition. The Personal Representative must inspect all that the Temporary Representative did, and raise objections if the Personal Representative does not approve of what was done (MGL 205:4A). Even if the same person serves in both capacities, it takes an extra step in the Probate procedure just to appoint a Temporary Representative. If you are asked to agree to the appointment of a Temporary Representative, you need to investigate the reason for the request and then come to your own conclusion as to whether such an appointment is necessary.

YOUR RIGHTS AS A BENEFICIARY

The Personal Representative is in charge of settling the Estate. Too often, beneficiaries of the Estate have no idea of what is going on. They wait to receive their inheritance, not knowing that they have rights under the law; and more importantly, not knowing how to assert their rights.

✧   RIGHT TO YOUR OWN ATTORNEY

The attorney who handles the Estate is employed by, and represents, the Personal Representative. If the Estate is sizeable, consider employing your own attorney to check that things are done properly and in a timely manner. Even with a small Estate, you may want to consult with an attorney if at any time you are concerned about the way the Probate is being conducted.

✧   RIGHT TO APPROVE PERSONAL REPRESENTATIVE

The person named as Executor of the decedent's Will has priority in being appointed as Personal Representative. If no Will, then the surviving spouse can serve or chose someone to do so. If there is no surviving spouse, the next of kin have the right to either serve as Personal Representative, or choose someone to do so (MGL 192:4, 193:1, 193:2).

If you have not agreed, in writing, to the appointment, then you should receive notice of the name and address of the person who is going to seek to be appointed as Personal Representative. If you have an objection to the person chosen to serve, then this is the time to raise those objections to the Probate Court. You can raise this, or any other objection you may have, without the assistance of an attorney, but it is best to consult with an attorney experienced in Probate matters before doing so.

The attorney will be able to explain the proper procedure to raise the objection. More importantly, the attorney will be able to tell you which arguments have a good chance of succeeding and which maybe doomed to failure and not worth pursuing.

✧ RIGHT TO COPY OF WILL

Within three months of his appointment, or of the date the Will is accepted into Probate, the Personal Representative must notify each beneficiary of what he is entitled to receive under the Will (MGL 192:12). If you have not seen a copy of the Will, you may want to call the Personal Representative or his attorney and request that a copy be forwarded to you.

✧ RIGHT TO DEMAND SUFFICIENT BOND

It doesn't happen often, but every now and again a Personal Representative will mismanage or run off with Estate funds. A bond that is backed by a surety company is insurance for the Estate. If Estate monies are lost or stolen then the surety company will reimburse the Estate for the loss. In Massachusetts, all Personal Representatives are required to be bonded, meaning they all agree to be liable for losses to the Estate due to their negligence, mismanagement or dishonesty. However, not all bonds need to be backed by a surety. The Court may exempt the surety requirement if:

⇨ the decedent's Will says that no bond is required; and
⇨ all of the heirs consent; and
⇨ all of the creditors are notified and given an opportunity to object to the absence of a surety. (MGL 205:1, 205:3, 205:4).

The cost of a surety bond is paid by the Estate, so ultimately the amount inherited is reduced by the amount paid for the bond. If you are asked to sign a release of the surety bond requirement, you need to consider whether you believe there is any risk of loss to the Estate. It is best not to sign the release, if you have such concern. Better to receive a little less, then nothing at all.

✧ RIGHT TO COPY OF INVENTORY

The Personal Representative must file an inventory of all of the assets of the Probate Estate. You can ask him or his attorney to give you a copy of the inventory as soon as it is filed with the Court. If you believe that the Estate was not correctly evaluated you can ask the Court to appoint a Special Appraiser (MGL 195:6, 205:1). Before making the request, consider consulting with your own attorney to explore the pros and cons of making the request. In particular, is the discrepancy in value significant enough to justify the cost of the appraisal?

✧ RIGHT TO AN ACCOUNTING

The beneficiaries of the Estate can require the Personal Representative to file an accounting anytime after a year has passed (MGL 206:1). The accounting should start with the inventory value of the Estate and end with the amount presently on hand. If the Estate has significant assets, you may want your own accountant to look at the accounting to be sure it is correct. If the Personal Representative refuses to do an accounting, then you can ask the Court to order him to do so. The Court could find that an accounting is not necessary at this point in time, so again it is best to consult with your attorney before bringing the matter before the Court. The Personal Representative is required to give a final accounting before any monies can be distributed. You will be given a copy of the accounting and an opportunity to raise any questions or concerns that you may have at that time (MGL 206:24).

✧ RIGHT TO APPROVE FEES

The Personal Representative is entitled to a reasonable fee for administering the Estate (MGL 206:16). If he is also a beneficiary of the Estate he may decide not to take a fee and just take his inheritance. The reason may be economic. Any fee the Personal Representative takes is taxable as ordinary income, but monies inherited are not taxable to him as a beneficiary. Ask the Personal Representative to tell you, in writing, whether he intends to ask for a fee, and if so, how much.

The Personal Representative has the right to employ an attorney to guide him through the procedure, and to have the attorney's fee paid with Estate funds. You, as a beneficiary, have the right to know how much will be charged for his services. Ask the Personal Representative to give you a copy of the retainer agreement, so that you will know how much is being charged for legal fees. If the attorney is employed on an hourly basis, have the attorney give a written estimate of the time he expects to expend on the Probate procedure.

There is no statutory guideline for what is a "reasonable" fee for the Personal Representative or for his attorney. The Massachusetts legislature has not set guidelines for what fees are considered to be reasonable, but Massachusetts Courts have ruled that when awarding fees, the Probate Court must take all of the facts into consideration including:
- ⇨ the size of the Estate
- ⇨ the legal questions involved
- ⇨ the time required to complete the work
- ⇨ the Personal Representative's skill and ability
- ⇨ the amount usually paid for similar work
- ⇨ the results accomplished

(*McMahon v. Krapf*, 323 Mass. 118, 80 N.E.2d 314 (1948).

Attorney's fees are also subject to the Court's approval. The Court will use much the same factors as above described to determine what represents a reasonable fee for the attorney (MGL 215:39A).

✧ RIGHT TO RECEIVE A DEBT FREE INHERITANCE

Once a beneficiary finally receives his inheritance, the last thing he wants to hear is that there is some unfinished business, or worse yet that monies need to be paid from the inheritance he received. But that is just what could happen if the Personal Representative distributes the money before all the creditors are paid. An unpaid creditor could sue the Personal Representative any time one year from the date of death. Once the year has passed, and the Probate Estate closed, a creditor can still seek payment by suing the beneficiaries of the Estate up to the value received by the beneficiary (MGL 197:9; 197:28, 197:29).

You can protect yourself from this unhappy situation by checking to see that all known creditors were notified of the death and of their right to file a claim. You should ask to see a copy of all of the tax returns that were filed, and then verify that any monies that were due have been paid. Most importantly, you should not agree to having the Estate closed if the closing statement shows that there are any outstanding debts that need to be paid.

IT'S YOUR RIGHT - DON'T BE INTIMIDATED

As a beneficiary, you have many legal rights, but you may feel uncomfortable asserting those rights with a friend or family member who is Personal Representative. Don't be. It's your money and your legal right to be kept informed. Be especially firm if the Personal Representative waves you off with:

"You've known me for years. Surely you trust me."

People who are trustworthy, don't ask to be trusted. They do what is right. The very fact that the Personal Representative is resisting, is a red flag. In such situation, you can explain that it is not a matter of trust, but a matter of what is your legal right.

At the same time, keep things in perspective. Your relationship with the Personal Representative may be more important to you than the money you inherit. The job of settling an Estate can be complex and demanding. If the Personal Representative is getting the job done, let him know you appreciate his efforts.

THE CHECK LIST

We have discussed many things that need to be done when someone dies in the state of Massachusetts. The next page contains a check list that you may find helpful.

You can check those items that you need to do, and then cross them off the list once they are done. We made the list as comprehensive as possible, so many items may not apply in your case. In such case, you can cross them off the list or mark them *N/A* (not applicable).

Things to do

FUNERAL ARRANGEMENTS TO BE MADE
☐ AUTOPSY   ☐ ANATOMICAL GIFT
☐ DISPOSITION OF BODY OR ASHES

DEATH CERTIFICATE
GIVE COPY TO: _____

_____

NOTICE OF DEATH
PEOPLE TO BE NOTIFIED _____

COMPANIES TO NOTIFY
☐ TELEPHONE COMPANY
    ☐ LOCAL CARRIER   ☐ LONG DISTANCE   ☐ CELLULAR
☐ NEWSPAPER (OBITUARY PRINTED)
☐ NEWSPAPER CANCELLED   ☐ deposit refund
☐ SOCIAL SECURITY
☐ INTERNET SERVER
☐ TELEVISION CABLE COMPANY
☐ POWER & LIGHT   ☐ deposit refund
☐ POST OFFICE
☐ OTHER UTILITIES (GAS, WATER)   ☐ deposit refund
☐ PENSION PLAN
☐ ANNUITY
☐ HEALTH INSURANCE COMPANY
☐ LIFE INSURANCE COMPANY
☐ HOME INSURANCE COMPANY
☐ MOTOR VEHICLE INSURANCE COMPANY
☐ CONDOMINIUM OR HOMEOWNER ASSOCIATION
☐ CANCEL SERVICE CONTRACT   ☐ **deposit refund**
☐ CREDIT CARD COMPANIES _____

    _____

    _____

Things to do

REMOVE DECEDENT AS BENEFICIARY OF:

☐ WILL ☐ INSURANCE POLICY ☐ PENSION PLAN
☐ BANK OR IRA ACCOUNT ☐ SECURITY

DEBTS

PAY DECEDENT'S DEBTS (AMOUNT & CREDITOR)

_____

COLLECT MONIES OWED TO DECEDENT (AMOUNT & DEBTOR)

_____

TAXES

☐ FILE FINAL FEDERAL INCOME TAX RETURN
☐ FILE FINAL STATE INCOME TAX RETURN
☐ RECEIVE INCOME TAX REFUND
☐ FILE ESTATE TAX RETURN

PROPERTY TO BE TRANSFERRED

☐ PERSONAL EFFECTS
☐ MOTOR VEHICLE
☐ BANK ACCOUNT
☐ CREDIT UNION ACCOUNT
☐ IRA ACCOUNT
☐ SECURITIES
☐ BROKERAGE ACCOUNT
☐ INSURANCE PROCEEDS
☐ REAL PROPERTY
☐ TIME SHARE
☐ CONTENTS OF SAFE DEPOSIT BOX

OTHER THINGS TO DO

_____
_____
_____

Once the Probate proceeding is over, you will be left with many documents and wonder which you need to keep:

COURT DOCUMENTS
You should keep a copy of the inventory to establish the value of property that you inherit. That value becomes your basis for any Capital Gains Tax that you may need to pay in the future. Other than the inventory, there is no reason to keep any Court document, provided you are satisfied with the way things were done; and do not intend to take action against the Personal Representative, or his attorney. The Clerk of the Probate Court keeps the Probate file on record, so if for some reason you later need a copy of a Probate document, you can get it from the Clerk.

PERSONAL RECORDS
The surviving spouse, or if no spouse, his next of kin should keep the decedent's personal papers (birth certificate, marriage certificate, naturalization papers, army records, religious documents, etc.). They may be needed in order to apply for government, or other, benefits. The next of kin may want to keep the decedent's medical records in the event that a family member needs to check out a genetic disease.

TAX RECORDS
The IRS has up to three years to collect additional taxes, and you have up to seven years to claim a loss from a worthless security, so you should keep the decedent's tax file for seven years from the date of filing the return. You can learn more about which records to keep from the IRS publication 552. You can get the publication by calling the IRS at (800) 829-3676 or you can download it from their Web site: http://www.irs.gov

Everyman's Estate Plan 7

The first six chapters of this book describe how to wind up the affairs of the decedent. As you read those chapters, you learned about the kinds of problems that can occur when settling the decedent's Estate. It is relatively simple for you to set up an Estate Plan so that your family members are not burdened with similar problems. An *Estate Plan* is the arranging of one's finances to reduce (if not eliminate) Probate costs and Estate taxes, and to ensure that your property is transferred quickly and at little cost.

If you think that only wealthy people need to prepare an Estate Plan, you are mistaken. Each year, heirs of relatively modest Estates, spend thousands of dollars to settle an Estate. A bit of planning could have eliminated most, if not all, of the expense and hassle suffered by those families.

The suggestions in this chapter are designed to assist the average person in preparing a practical and inexpensive Estate Plan, so we have named this chapter EVERYMAN'S ESTATE PLAN.

Once you create your own Estate Plan, you can be assured that your family will not be left with more problems than happy memories of you.

AVOIDING PROBATE

After reading the last Chapter, many will come to the conclusion that Probate is a good thing to avoid. Those who have $15,000 or less and no real property may not be concerned with avoiding Probate because as explained in the last chapter your beneficiaries can get possession of that property with little effort or expense.

But if you own real property, or property in excess of $15,000 in your name only, a full Probate will be necessary with all of its inherent delays and expenses. Notice that the operative phrase in the last sentence is *in your name only*. Whether a Probate procedure is necessary depends on how your property is titled (owned).

It makes no difference whether you do or do not have a Will. The determining factor is whether you own real property or personal property greater than $15,000, and that property is titled in your name only. In such case, your beneficiaries will need to go through Probate in order to get possession of that property.

As explained in Chapter 5, there are many ways to title real property so that it passes automatically without the need for Probate. For example, if you own real property jointly with rights of survivorship, upon your death, the survivors will own the property without the need to go through Probate. Similarly if you own a Life Estate, upon your death, the property passes directly to the remainder beneficiary.

In this Chapter we examine ways to title your personal property (bank accounts, securities, etc.) so that it passes to your beneficiaries without the need for Probate.

You can arrange to have all of your bank accounts set up so that should you die, the money goes directly to a beneficiary. For example, suppose all you own is a bank account and you want whatever you have in this account to go to your son and daughter when you die. You might think that a simple solution is to put each child's name on the account, but first consider the problems associated with a joint account:

⊠ **POTENTIAL LIABILITY**

If you hold a bank account jointly with your adult child and that child is sued or gets a divorce then the child may need to disclose his ownership of the joint account. In such a case, you may find yourself spending money to prove that the account was established for convenience only and that all of the money in that account really belongs to you.

⊠ **OVERREACHING**

If you set up a joint account with your child so that the child has authority to withdraw funds from the account, funds may be withdrawn without your authorization. If you open a joint account with two of your children, then after your death the first child to the bank may decide to withdraw all of the money, and that will, at the very least, cause hard feelings between them.

⊠ **THE MINOR CHILD**

In Massachusetts, a minor can own a savings or checking account alone or jointly with another. A minor can lease a safe deposit box in his name only or jointly with another (MGL 167D:7). But if you make a minor the joint owner of your account, would you want the child to be able to remove money from your account? Would you want the minor to be able to go to the bank and withdraw everything in your safe deposit box?

Because of these inherent problems, you might want to hold the funds so that your beneficiary does not gain access to the monies until and unless you die. There are two ways to do so: the "In Trust For" account, the "Pay On Death" account.

THE BENEFICIARY ACCOUNT

You can direct a financial institution to hold your account *In Trust For* ("ITF") a beneficiary that you name. During your lifetime you have complete control over the account. You can add to it or close it out entirely without permission from or notice to your beneficiary. The beneficiary does not have access to the account until you die (MGL 167D:6).

Massachusetts statute does not provide for a ITF account to be held for the benefit of more than one person. It may be that you wish to hold an account for the benefit of two or more beneficiaries. Your bank may offer other plans such as a *Pay On Death* ("POD") account. The terms of your agreement with the bank determines how the money in the account is to be distributed in the event of your death. For example, the account could be titled:

Eldon Connors POD Betty Connors and Fred Conners, JTWRS
This is short-hand for:
Eldon Connors Pay On Death to
Betty Connors and Fred Conners
as Joint Tenants With Rights of Survivorship.

The agreement with the bank will say that Eldon is the owner of the account, and that on his death, the money goes to Betty and Fred. If either of the beneficiaries of the account should die before Eldon, the account will go to the surviving beneficiary.

TRANSFER ON DEATH SECURITIES

In recent years there has been a blurring of the banking and securities industries. There are securities firms that operate much like a bank and vis-versa. Brokerage accounts, reinvestment or securities accounts can be set up to operate as a checking account with the owner of the account able to make cash withdrawals from the account.

A security or brokerage account can be registered so that the property is inherited by a beneficiary without the need for Probate. The account can be set up in beneficiary form by using the POD registration or the owner of the account can instruct the holder of security or brokerage account to *Transfer On Death* ("TOD") to a named beneficiary. With both the POD and TOD registration:

⇨ The beneficiary does not have access to the security or brokerage account until the owner dies.

⇨ During his lifetime the owner is free to change beneficiaries without asking the beneficiary's permission to do so.

For example, suppose a security or a brokerage account is titled: TANYA BEDDIE TOD JEB BEDDIE

Jeb does not have any right to the account while Tanya is alive. Once Tanya dies, all Jeb need do is produce a certified copy of the death certificate and the security or brokerage account will be transferred to him.
(MGL 201E: 102, 201E:106, 201E:107).

There may be times when you wish to hold a security or brokerage account jointly (say with your spouse) and have someone inherit the property when you both die. For example, if a brokerage account is titled:

TIM REILLY and OLIVIA REILLY, JT TEN
TOD TIM REILLY JR. AND SANDRA REILLY

⇨   Should either parent die, the surviving parent will own the account, and will be free to close it out or change the beneficiary of the account.

⇨   Once both parents are deceased, the children will share equally in the ownership of the account.

⇨   Should one of the children die, the surviving child will inherit the account once both parents are deceased.

⇨   If both children die before their parents, the account becomes part of the Estate of the last parent to die.

Massachusetts allows two or more people to hold a security or brokerage account in beneficiary form (POD or TOD), provided the owners of the account are Joint Tenants of the account. The law does not allow a beneficiary form if the owners of the account hold it as Tenants in Common; i.e. if a brokerage account is titled:

MARILYN STEWARD and JOAN STEWARD
as TENANTS IN COMMON.

Such an account cannot be held in beneficiary form. Should either owner of the account die, the share of the account that belongs to the decedent will become part of her Probate Estate (MGL 201E:103, 201E:401).

If your Estate consists only of bank accounts and/or securities, and you want all of your property to go to one or two beneficiaries without the need for Probate, but with maximum control and protection of your funds during your lifetime, holding your property in any one of these beneficiary forms: "In Trust For" "Pay-On-Death" "Transfer-On-Death" should accomplish your goal.

 NO CREDITOR PROTECTION

Property held in beneficiary form, i.e. ITF, POD or TOD account, does not belong to the beneficiary until the death of the owner of the account, and maybe not even then, if there is not enough money to pay for the monies owed by the decedent. Creditors of the owner of the account can demand that the monies in the account be used to pay claims against the decedent's Estate. The surviving spouse and children can require the account be used for to pay for allowances to which they are entitled under Massachusetts law. Such demands must be made in writing to the Personal Representative of the decedent's Estate within one year from the date of death (MGL 197:9, 201E:302, 201E:402).

The beneficiary of the decedent's account can take possession of the property, but would be wise not to spend the inheritance until the year has passed or until the beneficiary is sure that the Personal Representative does not need the money to settle the decedent's Estate.

If you are setting up a beneficiary account, and creditor protection is of concern to you, then the joint account might be a better way to go. As explained in Chapter 4, courts in Massachusetts have ruled that creditors cannot reach the decedent's funds if they are held jointly with rights of survivorship.

GIFT TO A MINOR CHILD

At the beginning of this chapter, we identified three problems with a joint account: potential liability if the joint owner is sued; overreaching by the joint owner, and holding an account jointly with a minor. The POD, TOD and ITF account each solve the problem of potential liability and overreaching, but if your beneficiary is a minor, there still is the problem of the child having access to a large sum of money. If the amount on deposit is small, the bank or financial institution may decide to turn the money over to the child's parent. For amounts of $10,000 or more, the company will seek Court approval before transferring the property (MGL 201A:7).

This presents a dilemma. If the amount given is no greater than $10,000, the parent can spend the money for the minor as he sees fit. The child may never even know of your gift. You may think it best that the child inherits more than $10,000; this way a Court will see to it that the monies are held safely till the child reaches 18. But that only presents a new set of problems. The Court will probably require a guardianship be set up to protect the funds. It takes time, effort and money to establish a guardianship. If you leave the child a significant amount of money, the Guardian has the right to charge to manage those funds. It could happen that the cost of the guardianship significantly reduces the amount of money inherited by the child.

There are ways to avoid the problem of having a Guardian appointed to care for property inherited by a child, and yet ensuring that the monies are protected. One method is to use the MASSACHUSETTS UNIFORM TRANSFERS TO MINORS ACT.

THE UNIFORM TRANSFERS TO MINORS ACT

The *Massachusetts Uniform Transfers to Minors Act* is designed to protect gifts made to a minor by appointing someone to be the *Custodian* of a gift until the child is an adult. For example, you can make a minor child the beneficiary of your life insurance policy, and name a trusted relative or friend or even a financial institution to be the Custodian of the gift. Should you die while the child is a minor, the insurance company will give the proceeds of the policy to the person you named as Custodian to hold until the child is an adult.

You can make a gift to a minor in your Will. You can appoint your Personal Representative (or anyone else) as Custodian of the gift. For example:

I give the sum of $20,000 to _____ (name) as custodian for _____ (name of minor) under the Massachusetts Uniform Transfers to Minors Act (MGL 201A:3, 201A:5).

THE LIFETIME GIFT

You can even use the Massachusetts Uniform Transfers to Minors Law to make a gift during your lifetime of some item such as shares in a corporation. You can nominate yourself as Custodian of the gift, or you can name another person to serve as Custodian. Once the lifetime gift is made it becomes irrevocable, so this method is not appropriate unless you are sure that you want the child to have the gift once he/she is an adult (MGL 201A:4, 201A:9).

In general, the Custodian must distribute the gift when the child reaches 18; however, if you make a lifetime gift, or a gift as part of your Will, you can direct the Custodian to distribute the gift when the child reaches 21 (MGL 201A:20).

The Custodian has the discretion to use the gift to care for the child. The Custodian can pay monies directly to the child, or can use the money for the child's benefit. The Custodian can refuse to use any of the monies for the child and just keep the property or funds invested until it is time to distribute the property. In such case, the child's guardian (or even the child once he/she is 14) can ask a Court to order that the monies be used for the care of the child. The Judge will determine what is in the child's best interest and then rule on the matter.

Hopefully, the Custodian will give a regular accounting to the child's guardian. If not, any member of the child's family, or the child once he/she reaches 14, can ask the Court to order a full accounting of the custodial property.

The law requires the Custodian to invest and manage the property in a responsible, prudent manner. The Custodian is entitled to be paid for his effort. If the gift is sizeable, then the Custodian's fee can be sizeable. Before appointing a person or a company as Custodian, it is best to come to a written agreement about how the property will be managed and the charge for doing so (MGL 201A:12, 201A:14, 201A:15, 201A:19, 201A:20).

The Uniform Transfers to Minors Act is good to use if you want a single gift to be given to a single person once he/she reaches the age of 21. If you want to provide for several children and have more flexibility about when they are to receive the gift, then a Trust may be the better way to go. We will discuss Trusts later in this chapter.

THE GIFT OF REAL PROPERTY

As explained in Chapter 5, if you own real property together with another, then who will own the property upon your death depends on how the Grantee is identified on the face of the deed. If you compare the Grantee clause of the deed to the examples given in Chapter 5 you can determine who will inherit that property should you die. If you are not satisfied with the way the property will be inherited, then you need to consult with an attorney to change the deed so that it will conform to your wishes.

If you hold real property in your name only, once you die, a Probate procedure will be necessary in order to transfer the property to the proper beneficiary. If your main objective is to avoid Probate, you can have an attorney change the deed so that it descends to your beneficiary without the need for Probate. As with bank and securities accounts there are different ways to do so, each with its own advantages and disadvantages.

JOINT OWNERSHIP

You can have your deed changed so that you and a beneficiary are joint owners with rights of survivorship. If you do so then should either of you die, the other will own the property 100%. That avoids Probate but you will not be able to sell that property during your lifetime without the beneficiary's permission. And if the beneficiary gives permission, the beneficiary will have the legal right to half of the proceeds of the sale. If the property is your homestead you may be creating a tax problem as well. You can arrange to sell your home without paying a Capital Gains Tax (see page 34), but if you make someone joint owner of your home, and they do not live there, a Capital Gains Tax may need to be paid on the joint owner's share of the proceeds of the sale.

CAUTION   GIFT OF HOME

Some elderly parents worry that they may need nursing care at some time in the future and lose all of their life savings to pay for that care. The parent may decide that the best way to avoid Probate and protect the homestead from loss is to transfer the homestead to their child with the understanding that the parent will continue to live there until he/she dies. But this is just trading risks:

☒ RISK OF LOSS

If you transfer your homestead to your child, it could be lost if the child runs into serious financial difficulties or gets sued. This is especially a risk if your child is a professional (doctor, nurse, accountant, financial planner, attorney, etc.). If your child is found to be personally liable for damages, then the house could become part of the settlement of that law suit.

A child who is (or gets) married complicates matters even more so. If the child is divorced, the property will need to be included as part of the settlement agreement. This may be to your child's detriment because the child may need to share the value of the property with his former spouse. If you do not transfer the property, it cannot become part of the marital equation.

⊠ LOSS OF HOMESTEAD CREDITOR PROTECTION

In Massachusetts, up to $300,000 of the value of your home is protected from your creditors (with the exception of mortgages, mechanic's liens and taxes) (MGL 188:1). If you are sued, and lose, you cannot be forced to sell your home unless the equity in your property is greater than $300,000. Even if you have sufficient equity and are forced to sell, at least you get to keep the first $300,000 of the proceeds. If you simply transfer your home to a child, you lose this protection. And the transfer of your home to a child may be a double loss of the homestead creditor protection if you are married. As explained in Chapter 4, this creditor protection continues for your surviving spouse should you die.

If the child does not occupy that property as his homestead, there is no homestead creditor protection whatsoever. The child's creditors can force the sale of the property (that's your home) for relatively small amounts of unpaid debts.

⊠ LOSS OF HOMESTEAD TAX EXEMPTION

Certain towns and cities in Massachusetts allow homestead tax credits or exemptions for certain residents, such as disabled servicemen, or parents of servicemen who lost their lives in wartime service or those who are blind or widowed, or over the age of 70 (MGL 59:5).

If you currently receive a tax exemption and you transfer the property, it could cost more money in taxes to continue to live in your own home.

⊠ POSSIBLE GIFT TAX

If the value of the transfer is worth more than $11,000 you need to file a gift tax return. For most of us, this is not a problem because no Gift Tax need be paid unless the value of the property (plus the value of all gifts in excess of the Annual Gift Tax Exclusion that you gave over your lifetime) exceeds $1,000,000 (see Page 37). If your Estate is in that tax bracket, .you need to be aware that you are "using up" your lifetime Gift Tax Exclusion.

⊠ POSSIBLE CAPITAL GAINS TAX

If you gift the property to the child, when he sells it he will be subject to a Capital Gains Tax on the increase in value from the price you paid to the selling price at the time of the sale. If you do not make the gift during your lifetime, the child will inherit the property with a step-up in basis, i.e., he will inherit the property at its market value as of the date of death. Under today's tax structure and continuing until 2009, that step-up in basis is unlimited. If your child sells the property when it is inherited, no Capital Gains Tax is due regardless of how large the step-up in basis. In 2010, there will be a limit on amount that can be inherited free of the Capital Gains Tax but that limit is high so for most of us this is not a concern.

Some of the problems associated with an outright gift, may be avoided by transferring the property to your child while keeping a Life Estate for yourself. But, as with joint ownership, you will not be able to sell or transfer the property during your lifetime unless your child agrees to the transfer. And as with joint ownership, should you sell the property your child is entitled to some part of the proceeds of the sale. Before deciding to transfer your homestead, it is important to consult with an attorney who can suggest other methods of avoiding Probate and protecting the homestead from loss.

⊠ POSSIBLE LOSS OF GOVERNMENT BENEFITS

If you transfer property, depending upon the value of the transfer, you could be disqualified from receiving Medicaid or Supplemental Security Income ("SSI") benefits for a substantial period of time. When a person applies for Medicaid, he must disclose whether, within three years of his application, he transferred property for less than the full value (i.e. he gifted the property).

This reporting period extends to five years if the transfer was to a Trust. The Medicaid agency will compute a disqualification period depending on the value of the transfer. This can present a serious problem should you need extended nursing care during that period of time.

Under current state and federal law, there are many ways to protect your homestead and still qualify for government benefits. Before transferring your homestead because of your concern for the cost of future health care, consult with an Elder Law attorney. He will be able to suggest ways to protect your assets, and still ensure that you receive the health care that you may require in your later years.

THE LIFE ESTATE, NOT A COMPLETE SOLUTION

Some of the problems we discussed regarding an outright gift of the homestead, can be avoided by transferring home but keeping a Life Estate for yourself. However, even though you keep a Life Estate, there still are tax issues and concerns regarding shared control of the property. Before making any transfer of real property, it is important to consult with an Elder Law attorney and/or certified financial planner and/or accountant, to examine all aspects related to the transfer.

Each state is in charge of the way property located in that state is transferred. If you own property in another state (or country), then you need to consult with an attorney in that state (or country) to determine how that property will be transferred to your beneficiaries once you die. The way property is transferred in Massachusetts, may not be the same as in the other state. For example, a deed held as Joint Tenants in Massachusetts, means that there are rights of survivorship, i.e., if one Joint Tenant dies, the remaining Joint Tenants own the property without the need for Probate. But other states may require that the deed specifically state that there are **rights of survivorship**.

In such states, property held as Joint Tenants is the same as holding property as Tenants In Common and a Probate procedure may be necessary in order to transfer the property. In such case, it may take two Probate procedures to settle your Estate. One in Massachusetts and another in the state where the property is located.

Still another problem is the matter of taxes. Massachusetts does not have an inheritance tax at this time, but another state may have an inheritance or transfer tax. Estate taxes may be due in the state where the property is located as well as in Massachusetts. It may be necessary to file a tax return in two states. In addition to increased taxes, this can double the cost of the accounting fees.

It is important to consult with an attorney for suggestions about how to set up your Estate Plan to avoid such problems.

A TRUST MAY BE THE SOLUTION (OR NOT)

A full Probate procedure may be necessary if you hold personal property in your name only that is worth more than $15,000, or if you hold real property as a Tenant-In-Common or in your name only. We explored different ways to re-title property to avoid Probate, but these methods may have trade-offs that are unacceptable to you. One way to avoid many of these potential problems is to set up a **Revocable Living Trust** (also known as an *Inter Vivos Trust*).

A Revocable Living Trust is designed to care for your property during your lifetime and then to distribute your property once you die without the need for Probate. You may have been encouraged to set up such a Trust by your financial planner, or attorney, or accountant. Even people of modest means are being encouraged to use a Trust as the basis of their Estate Plan. But Trusts also have their pros and cons. Before getting into that, let's first discuss what a Trust is and how it works:

SETTING UP A TRUST

To create a Trust, an attorney prepares the Trust document in accordance with the client's needs and desires. The person who signs the document is called the *Trustor* or *Settlor.* If the *Trustor* also funds the Trust, then he is also referred to as the *Grantor.* We will refer to the Revocable Living Trust as the "Living Trust" or just the "Trust" and the person setting up the Trust as the "Grantor." The Trust document identifies who is to be the Trustee (manager) of property placed in the Trust. Usually the Grantor appoints himself as Trustee so that he is in total control of property that he places into the Trust. The Trust document also names a Successor Trustee who will take over the management of the Trust property should the Trustee resign, become disabled or die.

Once the Trust document is properly signed, the Grantor transfers property into the Trust. The Grantor does this by changing the name on the account from his individual name to his name as Trustee. For example, if Elaine Richards sets up a Trust naming herself as Trustee, and she wishes to place her bank account into the Trust then all she need do is instruct the bank to change the name on the account from Elaine Richards to:

ELAINE RICHARDS, TRUSTEE OF THE ELAINE RICHARDS REVOCABLE TRUST AGREEMENT DATED JULY 12, 2004.

When the change is made, all the money in the account becomes Trust property. Elaine (wearing her Trustee hat) has total control of the account, taking money out, and putting money in, as she sees fit. Similarly, if she wants to put real property into the Trust all she need do is have her attorney prepare a new deed with the owner identified as ELAINE RICHARDS, TRUSTEE (see page 115 for an example of real property placed into a Trust).

The Trust document states how the Trust property is to be managed during Elaine's lifetime. Should Elaine become disabled the Trust will provide for her Successor Trustee to take over and manage the Trust property. Because the Trust is revocable, if she wishes, Elaine can terminate the Trust at any time and have all the Trust property placed back into her own individual name. If she does not revoke her Trust during her lifetime, then once she dies the Trust becomes irrevocable, and her Successor Trustee must follow the terms of the Trust Agreement as written. If the Trust says to give the Trust property to certain beneficiaries, the Successor Trustee will do so; and in most cases without the need for Probate. If the Trust directs the Successor Trustee to continue to hold property in Trust and use the money to take care of a member of Elaine's family, the Successor Trustee will do so.

THE GOOD PART
Setting up a Trust has many good features.

☆☆ AVOID PROBATE
The Massachusetts Probate procedure is relatively complex as compared to that of other states. Most state laws do not provide for the appointment of a Temporary Personal Representative. One person is appointed to serve as Personal Representative and unless something unusual happens, that person completes the job. But in Massachusetts, it is possible (although not probable) to have one person serve as Temporary Personal Representative and another as Personal Representative. Even if the same person serves as Temporary Personal Representative, and Personal Representative, a two-part Probate procedure can significantly increase the cost of Probate (MGL 201:1).

With or without the appointment of a Temporary Representative, the Probate procedure in Massachusetts can be both time-consuming and expensive. Owning property in more than one state also adds to the cost of Probate. It may be necessary to have a separate Probate procedure in each state. If you have a Trust that is properly drafted and you transfer your all of your assets (wherever located) into the Trust, you should be able to avoid Probate altogether.

☆ PRIVACY

Your Living Trust is a private document. No one but your Successor Trustee and your beneficiaries need ever read it. If you leave property in a Will and there is a Probate procedure, the Will must be filed with the Court, where it becomes a public document. Anyone can go to the courthouse, read your Will and see who you did (or did not) provide for in your Will. Records in the Probate Court (inventories, creditor's claims, etc.) are open to public scrutiny. In many states, Court records are now available on the Internet!

☆ CARE FOR A CHILD OR FAMILY MEMBER

You can make provision in your Trust to care for a child or family member after you die. If your family member is immature or a born spender, you can set up a Spendthrift Trust to protect him from squandering hid inheritance. You can direct your Successor Trustee to use Trust funds to pay for the family member's health care, education or living expenses, and nothing more.

NO CREDITOR PROTECTION FOR GRANTOR

Property that you hold in your Revocable Living Trust is freely accessible to you. It is likewise accessible to your creditors both before and after your death. If you die owing money, your Personal Representative can request that Trust funds be used to pay for those debts. If no Probate procedure is necessary, your creditor can demand payment from your Successor Trustee, provided the demand is made within one year from the date of your death (MGL 197:9).

☆☆   AVOID APPOINTMENT OF A GUARDIAN

Once you have a Trust you do not need to worry about who will take care of your property should you become disabled or too aged to handle your finances. The person you appoint as Successor Trustee will take over the care of the Trust property if you are unable to do so. If you do not make provision for the care of your property, it may be necessary for a Court to appoint a Guardian of your property. Guardianship is a good thing to avoid, not only because of the cost of the procedure, but also to avoid the embarrassment of a Court coming to the conclusion that you are not competent to manage your own finances.

Before appointing a Guardian, the Court will have a hearing to determine whether you are competent to manage your property. You are entitled to your own attorney at the hearing. If you do not have one the Court can appoint an attorney for you. If the Court determines that you do not have the capacity to handle your finances, he will appoint a Guardian. The Court will require the Guardian to obtain a bond for the protection of your property. Once appointed, the Guardian will take possession of your property and file an inventory with the Court. The Guardian will manage your property and each year account to the Court for monies spent. He may need to employ an accountant to assist with these reports. The Guardian needs to employ an attorney to establish the guardianship and see to it that it is properly administered. The Guardian, and his attorney are entitle to be paid for their efforts on your behalf (MGL 205:1, 205:5, 206:1, 215:39A).

Court filing fees, the cost of a bond, accounting fees, Guardian's fees, attorney's fees for you and the Guardian, are all paid from your Estate (that's your money!). And this expense goes on year after year until you are restored to capacity or die.

☆ FEDERAL ESTATE TAX SAVINGS

Many people think that the federal Estate Tax will be phased out so that by 2010, no Estate Taxes will be due regardless of the size of an Estate. But under current law in 2011, the Estate Tax is scheduled to be reinstated and those who own property worth more than $1,000,000 will once again be subject to a sizeable Estate Tax. A couple with an Estate in excess of a million dollars can reduce the risk of an Estate Tax by setting up a Trust, so that each partner can take advantage of his own Estate Tax Exclusion.

For example, if a couple own 2 million dollars, they can set up a Trust that separates the money into two Trusts once one partner dies. The Trust can be arranged so that the surviving spouse is free to use the income from both Trusts. Once both partners are deceased, the beneficiaries of their respective Trusts will inherit the funds, hopefully with no Estate Tax due.

If the couple do not set up a Trust and continue to hold all of their property jointly, the last to die will own the two million dollars with only one Estate Tax Exclusion available.

THE PROBLEMS

With all these perks, you may be ready to call your attorney to set up a Trust, but before doing so there are a few things you need to consider:

⊠ COMPLEXITY

A Trust is a fairly complex document, often 20 pages long. It needs to be that long because you are establishing a vehicle for taking care of your property during your lifetime, as well as after your death. The Trust usually is written in "legalese," so it may take you considerable time and effort to understand it. It is important to have your Trust document prepared by an attorney who has the patience to work with you until you fully understand each paragraph of the document and are satisfied that this is what you want.

⊠ PROBATE MIGHT STILL BE NECESSARY

The Trust only works for those items that you place in the Trust. If you purchase a security in your name only and without a "Transfer on Death" designation into your Trust, or to a beneficiary of your choice, a Probate procedure may be necessary to determine who should inherit the security. The attorney who prepares the Trust usually creates a safety net for such a situation by having you sign a "Pour Over Will" at the same time you sign your Trust.

The purpose of the Will is to "pour" any asset titled in your name only, into the Trust; specifically, the Will directs your Personal Representative to put any asset held in your name only into your Trust. This ensures that all of your property will go to the beneficiaries named in your Trust. But the downside is that a full Probate procedure may be necessary to get the asset into the Trust. This defeats a major goal of the Trust, namely to avoid Probate.

⊠ COST

Because of the thoroughness of the document and the fact that it is custom designed for you, a Trust will cost much more to draft than a simple Will. In addition to the initial cost of the Trust, it can be expensive to maintain the Trust should you become disabled or die. Your Successor Trustee has the right to charge for his duties as Trustee, as well as to charge for any specialized services performed. If you choose an attorney to be Successor Trustee, the attorney has the right to charge to manage the Trust, and also charge for any legal work he performs. A financial institution can charge to serve as Successor Trustee, and also charge to manage the Trust portfolio (MGL 206:16).

You can choose an attorney, or an accountant, or a financial planner, to serve as Trustee, but this creates a conflict of interest because the professional can use his position as Trustee to generate fees. If you decide to appoint a professional as Trustee you should have a fee agreement stating what will be charged for his duties as Trustee and what will be charged for professional work done on behalf of the Trust. The fee agreement should be be included in the Trust document with a provision that whoever accepts the job of Successor Trustee, agrees to accept the fee as provided in the Trust document. If you do not make written provision for fees, under Massachusetts law, the Trustee (and his attorney) are entitled to be compensated in the same manner as any fiduciary, such as a Personal Representative (MGL 215:39A).

You may decide to appoint your spouse or a family member as Successor Trustee, who may want little, or no, compensation. Regardless of who you choose to be Successor Trustee, you need come to a fee agreement. The agreement can be for a set amount or a percentage of the value of the Trust, or other method to be used to determine his compensation.

⊠ YOU MAY NEED YOUR SPOUSE'S PERMISSION
TO TRANSFER PROPERTY INTO YOUR TRUST

Most married couples prepare a Trust as part of their overall Estate Plan. Sometimes a married person has a Trust that was prepared prior to the marriage, or he may decide to create a Trust to care for children from a previous marriage. In such case, it may be necessary to have the spouse agree, in writing, to transfers into the Trust. The reason permission is needed is that in Massachusetts, your spouse owns Dower rights in all of your real property; that is a one-third Life Estate interest in all the real property you own as of your date of death (MGL 189:1). Your spouse has rights in your personal property as well, in the form of the Elective Share (see page 131) (MGL 191:15, 191:17).

Unless your spouse signed a prenuptial or postnuptial agreement giving up these rights, you will need permission from your spouse to transfer property into your Trust. If you make transfers into the Trust without your spouse's written permission, and without providing for the Dower rights or for the Elective Share, your surviving spouse can go to the Probate Court and demand that as much property be transferred from the Trust (or from anyone in possession of your property) as is necessary to make up for those Dower rights, or for the Elective Share.

⊠   TAXES MAY STILL BE A PROBLEM:

While the Grantor is operating the Trust as Trustee, all of the property held in a Revocable Living Trust is taxed as if the Grantor were holding that property in his/her own name. If the value of the Trust property exceeds the Estate Tax Exclusion and/or the Gift Tax Exclusion in effect at that time of the Grantor's death, taxes will be due and owing. For those in that fortunate tax bracket, an experienced Estate planner or tax attorney can suggest other, more advanced, Estate Planning strategies to reduce taxes.

⊠ ☆ THE TRUST IS LEGALLY ENFORCEABLE

Any beneficiary of the Trust can petition the Probate Court to settle a dispute arising out of the administration of the Trust. The Trustee also has the right to petition the Court for authority to do certain things not authorized in the Trust document. For example, the Trustee can ask the Court to issue an order giving the Trustee authority to terminate the Trust and distribute the Trust property to the beneficiaries (MGL 203:25, 215:6).

We gave this section a cross and a star, because the right to have a Trust enforced or administered by the Court is a double edged sword. It is great to have the Court protect the rights of your beneficiaries, but the cost of a Court battle could be greater than if your Estate was subject to Probate in the first place. Your beneficiaries are at a financial disadvantage. The Court can require your Trustee to be personally liable for legal costs, but that only happens if the Trustee acted illegally or unreasonably. In most cases, the Trustee will be able to charge the expense of defending his actions to your Trust and your beneficiaries will pay for their legal expenses out of their own pockets. Win or lose, there will be just that much less for your beneficiaries to inherit.

Although all of the methods discussed in this Chapter can be used to transfer property without the need for Probate, it may be each method has a downside that is objectionable to you. Maybe you don't have enough money to warrant the cost of setting up the Trust at this time. Holding property jointly with another may raise issues of security and independence. Holding property so that it goes directly to a few beneficiaries in a Pay On Death account, may not be as flexible as you wish.

This is especially the case if you wish to make gifts to several charities or to minor children instead of just one or two beneficiaries. For example, if you hold all your property so that it goes to your son without the need for Probate, and you ask him to use some of the money for your grandchild's education, it may be that your grandchild gets none of the money because your son is sued or falls upon hard times. If you keep your property in your name only and leave a Will giving a certain amount of money for your grandchild, the child will know exactly how much money you left and the purpose of that gift.

After taking into account all the pros and cons of avoiding Probate, you may well opt for a Will and a Probate procedure. If you make such a decision, it is important to keep in mind that Estate Planning is not an "all or nothing" choice. You can arrange your Estate so that certain items pass automatically to your intended beneficiary, and other items can be left in your name only, to be distributed as part of a Probate procedure. By arranging your finances in this manner, you can reduce the value of your Probate Estate, and that in turn should reduce the cost of Probate.

Your Massachusetts Will 8

Many people decide that the Will is the best route to go but do not act upon it, thinking it unnecessary to prepare a Will until they are very old and about to die. But according to reports published by the National Center for Health Statistics (a division of the U.S. Department of Health and Human Services) 2 of every 10 people who die in any given year are under the age of 60.

Twenty percent may seem like a small number until it hits close to home as it did with a young couple. They were having difficulty conceiving a child. They went from doctor to doctor until they met someone just beginning his practice. With his knowledge of the latest advances in medicine, he was able to help them.

The birth of their child was a moment of joy and gratitude. They asked a nurse to take a picture of them all together — the proud parents, the newborn child and the doctor who made it all possible. Happiness radiated from the picture, but within 6 months, one of them would be dead.

You might think it was the child. An infant's life is so fragile. SIDS and all manner of childhood diseases can threaten a little one. But no, he grew up a healthy young man.

If you looked at the picture, you might guess the husband. Overweight and stressed out; his ruddy complexion suggested high blood pressure. He looked like a typical heart- attack-prone type A personality.

No, he was fine and went on to enjoy raising his son.

Probably the wife. She had such a difficult time with the pregnancy and the delivery was especially hard. Perhaps it was all too much for her. No, she recovered and later had two more children.

It was the doctor who was killed in a collision with a truck.

WHY A WILL IS NECESSARY

Though we all agree, that one never knows, still people put off making a Will figuring that if they die before getting around to it, Massachusetts law will take over and their property will be distributed in the manner that they would have wanted anyway. The problem with that logic is the complexity of the Massachusetts Laws Of Descent. It isn't too difficult to figure out who will inherit your property if you are survived by a spouse, child, parent or sibling. But if none of these survive you, the ultimate beneficiary of your property may not be the person you would have chosen, had you taken the time to do so.

Others think that it is not necessary to have a Will because they have arranged their finances so that all of their property will be inherited without the need for Probate. But money could come into your Estate after your death. This could happen in any number of ways from winning the lottery and dying (of happiness, no doubt) to receiving insurance funds after your death. For example, if you die in a house fire or flood the insurance company may need to pay for damage done to your property. In such case, a Personal Representative may need to be appointed and the monies distributed according to Massachusetts law.

If you die without a Will, the Personal Representative may not be the person you would have chosen. The monies may be distributed differently than you would have wished. And as explained in this Chapter, there are other important reasons to make a Will.

SET PERSONAL REPRESENTATIVE'S FEE

Another reason to make a Will is so that you can come to an understanding with your Personal Representative about how much compensation he is to receive to settle your Estate. You can state that value in your Will.

THE PERSONAL REPRESENTATIVE
CAN SEEK MORE MONEY

Your Personal Representative might find that the job was more complicated than he expected and decided to ask for more money than you specified in the Will. It is up to the Probate Court to approve the amount paid for the Personal Representative's fee. The Court may think that the amount stated in the Will was the amount you wanted to spend, but not necessarily the amount agreed to by your Representative.

To avoid the problem, you can have your attorney draft a binding agreement signed by you and your Personal Representative and attach it to your Will. This will not prevent your Representative from asking the Court for more money, but with such an agreement, it will be harder to get the Court to agree to the increase.

You also need to keep in mind that the Personal Representative's fee is just to administer the Estate. It does not include payment for professional work he may do while settling the Estate. For example, if you appoint your attorney as Personal Representative, he can agree to the amount stated in the Will for his role as Personal Representative, and then ask the Court to award him attorney's fees as well. The same goes for any other professional. A financial planner who serves as Personal Representative may be compensated for his management of the Estate property (buying and selling securities, taking care of rental property, etc.) in addition to his fee to administer the Estate. An accountant who serve as Personal Representative, is entitled to receive compensation for his work as Personal Representative and also for any accounting work he does such as preparing and filing tax returns; preparing an inventory and accounting to the beneficiaries.

But the main problem with appointing a professional as your Personal Representative is the same as appointing a professional to serve as the Successor Trustee of your Trust; namely, that it creates a potential conflict of interest. The professional might use his position as Personal Representative to generate fees that may not have been necessary had someone else be settling the Estate.

Unless the professional is the sole beneficiary of your Estate, it is better to chose a non-professional for the job.

▤   CHOOSE A GUARDIAN FOR YOUR MINOR CHILD

Each parent has the right to name someone in their Will to be Guardian of their child in the event that the parent dies before the child is grown, and the other parent is deceased. The Judge will honor your choice of Guardian unless it would not be in the best interest of the child to do so (MGL 201:2).

▤   MAKE ADJUSTMENT FOR PRIOR GIFTS

You can make adjustments in your Will for gifts or loans given during your lifetime. For example, if you have loaned money to a family member and do not expect to be repaid, you can deduct the loan from that person's inheritance. There is no need to make the adjustment if the borrower gives you a promissory note because should you die, the monies will be owed to your Estate and the Personal Representative can deduct the monies owed from the borrower's inheritance. But if there is no evidence of the debt and you neglect to make a Will, the borrower will receive whatever is allowed under the Laws of Intestate Succession.

📑 MAKE GIFTS OF YOUR PERSONAL PROPERTY

Another benefit of making a Will is that you can make provision for who will get your personal property, including your car. If you make a gift of your car in your Will, then it will be relatively simple for your car to be transferred to the beneficiary. If you do not make a specific gift of your car, then it becomes part of your residuary Probate Estate. Your Personal Representative will decide what to do with the car. He can sell it and include the proceeds of the sale in the Estate funds to be distributed to your residuary beneficiaries; or he can give the car to one beneficiary of your Estate as part of that beneficiary's share of the Estate.

SMALL GIFTS MATTER

Many who have lost someone close to them report that the distribution of small personal items caused the greatest conflict. If you arrange your finances so that no Probate procedure is necessary, your next of kin will need to decide how to distribute your personal effects. Without guidance from you and no Personal Representative with authority to make decisions, there could be disagreement and hard feelings, over items of little monetary value. If you make a Will, you can include a list of gifts of personal effects in your Will and your Personal Representative will distribute the gifts according to your directions.

Of course, you cannot list each and every item you own, but you can instruct your Personal Representative to allow certain family members to take their choice of items not mentioned in your Will. If two or more family members want the same item, then have your Personal Representative use an appropriate lottery system (coin toss, high card in a cut of a deck of cards, etc.) to decide who "wins."

Some people think that preparing a Will is a simple thing — something they can do themselves. But writing a Will is like figure skating. It is harder than it looks. A Will needs to be clearly worded. A sentence that can be read in two different ways can lead to a dispute over what you intended; and that could result in a long and expensive Court battle. The Will must be signed and witnessed according to Massachusetts law, otherwise the Judge may refuse to admit the Will to Probate, and your property will be distributed as if you had no Will at all.

Unless you take the time to make yourself knowledgable about Massachusetts law as it relates to Wills, it is best to have an attorney who is experienced in Estate Planning, prepare one for you. As explained in Chapter 5, there are any number of reasons to challenge a Will. If you want to be assured that your Will is honored, it is best to have an Estate Planning attorney, prepare a Will according to your directions and then supervise the signing of your Will.

Once you sign your Will, you may wonder where to store it. Your attorney may suggest that he place it in his vault for safekeeping. By doing so, he ensures that your heirs will need to contact him as soon as you die. This does not mean that they are required to employ him should a Probate proceeding be necessary. It only means that he will have an opportunity for future employment.

But there are problems with such an arrangement. The Will could be lost or mistaken for another Will. That happened in at least one case. The attorney prepared Wills for two people with the same name and similar family circumstances. When one person died the attorney submitted the wrong Will to Probate.

If you decided to allow your attorney to store the Will, you need assurances that the attorney will be responsible for the document. You should get a receipt and something in writing that says:

⇨   The attorney accepts full responsibility for the storage of the Will. Should it be lost or damaged, he will replace the document at no cost to you; and if you are deceased, he will, at no cost to your heirs, present sufficient evidence to the Court to accept a valid copy of the Will into Probate.

⇨   There will be no charge to you, or your heirs, for the storage and retrieval of the document.

⇨   Should he sell his practice, retire, or die, he or the successor to his practice, will return the original document to you.

THE SAFE DEPOSIT BOX — SAFE BUT . . .
You might consider placing your Will in a safe deposit box that you lease at a bank. The only problem with the bank safe deposit box is convenient access. If you hold a safe deposit box in your name only, should you die, the bank will restrict access to the safe deposit box. The bank may, but is not required to, allow a family member to inspect the contents of the box. In many cases, the bank will not allow access without Court authority.

Once a Personal Representative is appointed by the Court, he will have such authority and be able to remove the contents of the safe deposit box. But if you arranged your finances to avoid Probate, then it is self defeating to have entry to a safe deposit box trigger a Probate procedure.

For those who are married, the solution to the problem of accessing the safe deposit box after death, is to lease the box jointly with your spouse, such that each of you have free access to the box. Those who have a Trust can solve the problem by leasing the safe deposit box in their capacity as Trustee, and giving their Successor Trustee joint access to the safe deposit box.

If you are single and do not have a Trust, you can lease the box jointly with a trusted family member. Of course, if privacy and security are important to you, then this might offset any concern for the convenience of your beneficiaries.

STORE IT WITH THE COURT

Perhaps the best solution is to store your Will with the Register of Probate in the county of your residence. The fee for doing so is nominal (currently $5) (MGL 191:10). You are free to retrieve the Will from the Register in the event that you move or decide to change your Will.

Regardless of where you choose to store your Will, let your Personal Representative know that you have a Will and how to retrieve it in the event of your death.

CHOOSING THE RIGHT ESTATE PLAN

Joint Ownership?
A POD Account?
A TOD Security?
A Trust?
A Will?
An Insurance Policy???

Chapters 7 and 8 offer so many options that the reader may be more confused than when he was blissfully unenlightened.

As with most things in life, you may find there are no ultimate solutions, just alternatives. The right choice for you is the one that best accomplishes your goal. This being the case, you first need to determine what you want to accomplish with the money you leave. Think about what will happen to your property if you were to die suddenly, without making any plan different from the one you now have.

      Who will be responsible to pay your bills?
      Who will get your property?
      Will Probate be necessary?

If the answers to these questions are not what you wish, then you need to work to arrange your property to accomplish your goals.

For those with significant assets, — especially those with Estates large enough to pay Estate taxes, a trip to an experienced Estate Planning attorney may be well worth the consultation fee.

Your Estate Plan Record　9

Once you are satisfied with your Estate Plan, then the final thing to consider is whether your heirs will be able to locate your assets once you are deceased.

Most people have their business records in one place, their Will in another place, car titles and deeds in still another place. When someone dies, their beneficiaries may feel as if they are playing a game of "hide and seek" with the decedent. The game might be fun were it not for the fact that an unlocated item may be forever lost. For example, suppose you die in an accident and no one knows you are insured by your credit card company for accidental death in the amount of $25,000. The only one to profit is the insurance company, which is just that much richer because no one told them that you died as a result of an accident.

And how about a key to a safe deposit box located in another state? Will anyone find it? Even if they find the key, how will they find the box?

It is not difficult to arrange things so that your affairs are always in order. It amounts to being aware of what you own (and owe) and keeping a record of your possessions. A side benefit is that by doing so, you will always know where all your business records are. If you ever spent time trying to collect information to file your taxes or trying to find a lost stock or bond certificate, you will appreciate the value of organizing your records.

Heirs need all the help they can get. It is difficult enough dealing with the loss, without the frustration of trying to locate important documents. Your heirs will have no problem locating your assets if you keep all of your records in a single place. It can be a desk drawer or a file cabinet or even a shoe box. It is helpful if you keep a separate file or folder for each type of investment. You might consider setting up the following folders:

📁 THE BANK & SECURITIES FOLDER

Store your original certificates for stocks, bonds, mutual funds, certificates of deposit, in a folder labeled BANK & SECURITIES FOLDER. In addition to the original certificate include a copy of the contract you signed with each financial institution. The contract will show where you have funds and who you named as beneficiary or joint owner of the account. If someone owes you money and has signed a promissory note or mortgage that identifies you as the lender, then you can store these documents in this folder as well.

If you store your original documents in a safe deposit box, keep a record of the location of the safe deposit box, and the number of the box, in this folder. Make a copy of all of the items stored in the box and place the copies in this folder. If you have an extra key to the box, put it in the folder. If you are the only person with access to the box, it may take a Probate procedure to remove items from the box once you die. Consider leasing the box so that someone you trust will be able to gain entry to the box in the event of your incapacity or death.

🗀 THE INSURANCE FOLDER

The INSURANCE FOLDER is for each original insurance policy that you own, be it life insurance, health insurance, car insurance or a homeowner's insurance policy. If you purchased real property, you may have received a title commitment at closing and the original title insurance policy some weeks later when you received your original deed from recording. If you cannot locate the title insurance policy, contact the closing agent and have him send you a copy of your title policy.

🗀 THE PENSION AND ANNUITY FOLDER

If you have a pension or annuity, put all of the documents relating to the Pension in this folder. Include the telephone number and/or address of the person to contact in the event of your death.

FOR FEDERAL RETIREES If you are a Federal Retiree, you should have received your **PERSONAL IDENTIFICATION NUMBER (PIN)** and the person who will inherit your pension (your *survivor annuitant*) should have received his own PIN as well. It is relatively simple to obtain this during your lifetime, but it may be difficult and stressful for your survivor annuitant to work through the system once you are gone.

Survivor annuitant benefits are not automatic. Your survivor annuitant must apply for them by submitting a death claim to the Office of Personnel Management. Your survivor needs to know that it is necessary to apply and also how to apply. You can get printed information about how apply for benefits from the Office Of Personnel Management (see Page 30). Keep the information in this file.

🗁   THE DEED FOLDER

Many people save every scrap of paper associated with the closing of real property. If you closed recently on real estate and there was a mortgage involved in the purchase, you probably walked away from closing with enough paper to wallpaper your kitchen. If you wish, you can keep all of those papers in a separate file that identifies the property, for example:
CLOSING PAPERS FOR THE QUINCY PROPERTY

Place the original deed (or a copy if the original is in a safe deposit box) in a separate DEED FOLDER. Include cemetery deeds, condominium deeds, cooperative shares to real property, timesharing certificates, deed to out of state property, etc. Also include a copy of related documents such as an Abstract of Title, or a recorded Condominium Approval. If you have a title insurance policy, put the original in the insurance folder, and a copy in this folder. If you have a mortgage on your property, put a copy of the mortgage and promissory note in a separate LIABILITY FOLDER.

LOCATING REAL PROPERTY

If you own a vacant lot, your beneficiaries will find the deed (or a copy) in this folder but that deed will not contain the address of that property because it doesn't have one. The post office does not assign a street address until there is a building on the site. Your beneficiaries can get the location of the property from city or county records. But why make things hard for them? Include a simple handwritten note in this folder that tells them exactly how to locate the property.

📁 THE LIABILITY FOLDER

The LIABILITY FOLDER should contain all loan documents of debts that you owe. For example, if you purchased real property and have a mortgage on that property, put a copy of the mortgage and promissory note in this folder. If you owe money on a car, put the loan documents in this folder. If you have a credit card, put a copy of the contract you signed with the credit card company in this folder.

Many people never take the time to calculate their net worth (what a person owns less what that person owes). By having a record of your assets and outstanding debts, you can calculate your net worth whenever you wish.

📁 THE ESTATE PLANNING DOCUMENT FOLDER

Place your Will and/or Trust in a separate folder. If your attorney has your original Will, make a note of that fact together with a copy of the Will. If you deposited the original Will with the Register of Probate, then put your Certificate of Receipt in this folder. If the original document is in a safe deposit box, place a copy of the document in this folder together with instructions about how to find the original. It is important to keep a copy of your Will or Trust in this folder because over the years you may forget what provision you made. Keeping a copy in your home may save you a trip to the safe deposit box to determine whether you need to update the document.

If you made burial or funeral arrangements, you can keep those documents in this folder

THE PERSONAL PROPERTY FOLDER

MOTOR VEHICLES

Put all motor vehicle titles in a Personal Property folder. This includes cars, mobile homes, boats, planes, etc. If you owe money on the vehicle, the lender may have possession of the title certificate. If such is the case, put a copy of the title certificate and registration in this folder and a copy the loan documents in a separate liability folder. If you have a boat or plane, then identify the location of the motor vehicle. For example, if you are leasing space in an airplane hangar or in a marina, keep a copy of the leasing agreement in this file.

JEWELRY

If you own expensive jewelry, keep a picture of the item together with the sales receipt or written appraisal in this folder.

COLLECTOR'S ITEMS

If you own a valuable art or coin collection, or any other item of significant value, include a picture of the item in this file. Also include evidence of ownership of the item, such as a sales receipt or a certificate of authenticity, or a written appraisal of the property.

🗁 THE PERSONAL RECORDS FOLDER

The PERSONAL RECORDS FOLDER should include documents that relate to you personally, such as a birth certificate, naturalization papers, pre-nuptial or post-nuptial agreement, marriage certificate, divorce papers, military records, social security card; etc. If you have a Health Care Proxy, or a Durable Power of Attorney, you can place them in this folder or your Estate Planning folder. If you placed the original document in a safe deposit box, then keep a copy in this folder together with the location of the original.

🗁 THE TAX RECORD FOLDER

Your Personal Representative (or next of kin) will need to file your final income tax returns. Keep a copy of your tax returns (both federal and state) for the past three years in your Tax Record Folder.

As explained in Chapter 2, beginning in 2010, there will be a cap on the step-up basis to 4.3 million dollars for property inherited by the spouse and 1.3 million dollars for property inherited by anyone else. It is important to keep a record of the basis of your property, not only for your heirs, but yourself should you decide to sell the property during your lifetime. If you purchase real property, you need to keep a record of the purchase price as well as monies you paid to improve the property. You will need these records to determine whether there will be a Capital Gains Tax on the transfer. Your accountant can help you set up a bookkeeping system to keep a running record of your basis in everything you own of value.

THE *If I Die* FILE

Many do not have the time, nor inclination, to "play" with all these folders. They do not anticipate an immediate demise. Getting hit by a truck, or dying in a fiery plane crash is not something to think about, much less prepare for. But consider that death is not the only problem. You could take suddenly ill (say with a stroke) and become incapacitated. Even the most time-starved optimist should have a murmur of concern that his loved ones will be left with a mess should something unforeseen happen.

If you do not feel like doing a complete job of organizing your records at this time, consider an abridged version. You can set up a single file with a list of all you own and the location of each item. You need to make that file easily accessible to whomever you wish to manage your affairs in the event of your incapacity or death. You can do this by letting that person know of the existence of the file and how to get it in an emergency; or keep the file in an easily accessed place in your home with the succinct but attention-grabbing title of "*If I Die.*"

We have included a form on the next page that you can use as a basis for information to be included in the file.

If I Die

then the following information will help settle my estate:

INFORMATION FOR DEATH CERTIFICATE

MY FULL LEGAL NAME _____

MY SOCIAL SECURITY NO. _____

MY USUAL OCCUPATION _____

BIRTH DATE AND BIRTH PLACE _____

If naturalized, date & place _____

MY FATHER'S NAME _____

MY MOTHER'S MAIDEN NAME _____

PERSONS TO BE NOTIFIED

_____

_____

_____

FUNERAL AND BURIAL ARRANGEMENTS

LOCATION OF BURIAL SITE

_____

LOCATION OF PREPAID FUNERAL CONTRACT

_____

FOR VETERAN or SPOUSE BURIAL IN A NATIONAL CEMETERY

BRANCH_____SERIAL NO._____

VETERAN'S RANK _____

VETERAN'S VA CLAIM NUMBER _____

DATE AND PLACE OF ENTRY INTO SERVICE:

_____

DATE AND PLACE OF SEPARATION FROM SERVICE:

_____

LOCATION OF OFFICIAL MILITARY DISCHARGE
OR DD 214 FORM_____

LOCATION OF LEGAL DOCUMENTS

BIRTH CERTIFICATE _____

MARRIAGE CERTIFICATE_____

DIVORCE DECREE _____

PASSPORT _____

WILL OR TRUST _____

DEEDS _____

MORTGAGES _____

TITLE TO MOTOR VEHICLES _____

HEALTH CARE DIRECTIVES _____

Name, telephone of attorney _____

LOCATION OF FINANCIAL RECORDS

INSURANCE POLICIES:

Name of Company, Location of Policy, Insurance Agent

_____

_____

PENSIONS/ANNUITIES:

IF FEDERAL RETIREE: PIN NUMBER: _____

NAME OF SURVIVOR _____

SURVIVOR PIN NUMBER _____

BANK

Name and address of Bank, Account Number,
Location of Safe Deposit Box and Key

_____

_____

SECURITIES

Name and telephone number of broker

_____

TAX RECORDS FOR PAST 3 YEARS

LOCATION _____

Name and telephone number of accountant

_____

KEEPING UP TO DATE

We discussed people's natural disinclination to make an Estate Plan until they are faced with their own mortality. Many believe that they will make just one Will and then die (maybe that's why they put off making a Will). The reality is, most people who make a Will change it at least once before they die. If you have an Estate Plan, it is important to update it when any of the following events take place:

✍ A CHANGE IN RELATIONSHIP

If you marry, divorce, have a child, or if a beneficiary of your Estate dies, you need to examine your Estate Plan to determine whether it needs to be revised. If you decide that your Will needs a complete revision, then it is important to have a new Will prepared. If you simply rip up the old Will, that will effectively revoke the Will. But it could happen that someone (perhaps your attorney) has a copy of the Will. If no one knows that you revoked the Will, they may think the Will is lost and then offer the copy of the Will for Probate (see page 76). If you draft a new Will, then the first paragraph should say, "I revoke all prior Wills ..."

BENEFICIARY MOVES OR DIES Most people remember to name an alternate beneficiary should one of their beneficiaries die. But how many of us remember to notify the pension plan or insurance company when a beneficiary moves? Many life insurance proceeds are never paid because the company cannot locate the beneficiary. The Actuarial Office of the Federal Employees' Group Life Insurance Program reported that as of October, 2001, they had over 40 million dollars in unpaid benefits, mostly because they could not locate the beneficiary at the last given address.

✍ CHANGE IN MARITAL STATUS

If your marry or divorce, there are certain changes that take place by law. For example, if you divorce and die before you get around to changing your Will, any provision that you made for your former spouse is read as if he/she died before you (MGL 191:9). But it is important to not just rely on the law. Best to change all documents after a divorce or separation. This includes deeds, Health Care Proxy, Power of Attorney, etc.

NOTIFY EMPLOYER OF CHANGE IN RELATIONSHIP

If you change your marital status you need to tell your employer of the change so that the employer can change your status for purposes of paycheck deductions, health insurance coverage, and change of beneficiary for your Pension Plan. As explained in Chapter 6, up to $100 in wages can to be transferred to your spouse. If you change your marital status, notify your employer, in writing, who is to receive your unpaid wages in the event of your death.

✍ RELOCATION TO A NEW STATE OR COUNTRY

There is no need to change your Estate Plan for a move within state. If you change your county of residence and you deposited your original Will with the Register of Probate, you need to retrieve that Will and deposit it with the Register in the county of your new residence. Similarly, if you move to a new state, you need to retrieve your Will from the Register of Probate and take it with you to the new state. Not every state allows the deposit of a Will prior to the death of the Will maker. You may need to make other arrangements to store your Will in the new state.

If your attorney has your original Will or any other original of your Estate Planning documents, then unless you plan to keep him as your lawyer, you need to retrieve these items to take with you to the new state.

If you have a Will or Trust, and you are married, you need to determine whether your Will conforms to the laws of the state of your new residence. Most states will honor a Will drafted according to Massachusetts law, however, the rights of a spouse vary considerably state to state. If you are married and have not provided the minimum amount as required by the laws of the new state, should you die before your spouse, your Will may be challenged on that basis. The same applies to a Trust. Most states allow a surviving spouse to demand funds from the Trust of the decedent spouse, if the deceased spouse did not provide the minimum amount to his spouse as required by the laws of that state.

Each state has its own, unique, Laws of Descent and Distribution. In many state they are called the *Laws of Intestate Succession.* Who has the right to inherit your property in the Commonwealth of Massachusetts may be different from who will inherit your property in another state. If you do not have a Will, then this is the time to think about who will get your property in the state of your new residence. This is especially important for those who are married. The right of a spouse to inherit property varies significantly from state to state. There is a world of difference between the rights of a spouse in a community property state and other states. And there is even variation in the rights of a spouse from one community property state to another!

You also need to check out the taxes of the new state. Each state has its own tax structure. Some states have an inheritance tax, or a transfer tax on all inherited property. If state taxes are high, you may need an Estate Plan that will minimize the impact of those taxes.

OTHER ESTATE PLANNING DOCUMENTS

If you appointed a Health Care Agent under a Health Care Proxy, you need to determine whether the document will be honored in the new state. Laws relating to health care vary significantly. Other states may not have laws providing for the appointment of a Health Care Agent, but they may have laws that enable you to appoint a *Patient Advocate* or a *Health Care Surrogate* or a *Health Care Representative*, with the right to make your health care decisions in the event that you are too ill to do so yourself. It is best to sign a new health care document using the forms and terms recognized in that state, rather than chance any confusion should you become ill and find yourself in an emergency situation.

Similarly, if you appointed someone to handle your finances under a Power of Attorney, you need to determine whether that document will be honored in the new state.

CREDITOR PROTECTION

Creditor protection is another item that is significantly different state to state. If you have much debt, then determine what items can be inherited by your family free of your debts.

When moving to another state you need to either educate yourself about the laws of the state, or consult with an attorney who can assist you in reviewing your Estate Plan to see if that plan will accomplish your goals in that state.

✍ A SIGNIFICANT CHANGE IN THE LAW

We pay our legislators (state and federal) to make laws and, if necessary, change those in effect. We pay judges to interpret the law and that interpretation may change the way the law operates. The legislature and the judiciary do their job and so laws change frequently. Tax laws are particularly volatile. The 2001 change in the Federal Estate Tax law gradually increases the Exclusion amount so that by 2010 no Federal Estate Tax will be due regardless of the value of your Estate. You may be thinking that there is no need for an Estate Tax plan because you don't intend to die prior to 2010. But any certainty relating to death and taxes is false security (especially taxes, in this case). As explained in Chapter 2, the law as passed in 2001, is effective only until December 31, 2010. If lawmakers do nothing, then on January 1, 2011, the Federal Estate Tax goes back into effect; and Estates that exceed one million dollars will once again be subject to Estate taxes.

And that is not the only uncertainty. Each state has its own Estate Tax structure. It remains to be seen how each state will react to the federal change. Some states may follow the lead of the federal government and increase their Estate Tax Exclusion in the same manner. Other states may see this as an opportunity to "pick up the slack" i.e., to increase their Estate Taxes, so that monies that would have been paid to the federal government will now be paid to the state.

You need to keep up with the news to learn about changes in the law that affect your Estate Plan. It is a good idea to check with your attorney on a regular basis to see if any change in the state or federal law affects your current Estate plan. And also check out the Eagle Publishing Company Web site for changes we will post to keep this book fresh.   http://www.eaglepublishing.com

GAMES DECEDENTS PLAY

We discussed the game of "hide and seek" some decedents play with their heirs. A variation of that game is the "wild goose chase." The person who plays this game is one who never updates his files. His records are filled with all sorts of lapsed insurance policies, promissory notes of debts long since paid; brokerage statements of securities that have been sold, and so on.

When he is gone, his family will become frustrated as they try to hunt down the "missing" asset. If you wish to play this game, then the best joke is to keep the key to a safe deposit box that you are no longer leasing. That will keep folks hunting for a long time!

If you do not have a wicked sense of humor, then do your family a favor and update your records on a regular basis.

Glossary

ABSTRACT OF TITLE   An *Abstract of Title* is a condensed history of the title to the land, consisting of a summary of all of the recorded documents that affect the land, including mortgages.

ADMINISTRATION The *administration* of a Probate Estate is the management and settlement of the decedent's affairs. There are different types of administration. See *Ancillary Administration* and *Summary administration.*

AFFIANT   An *Affiant* is someone who signs an affidavit and swears that it is true in the presence of a notary public or person with authority to administer an oath.

AFFIDAVIT   An *Affidavit* is a written statement of fact made by someone voluntarily and under oath, in the presence of a notary public or someone who has authority to administer an oath.

AGENT   An *Agent* is someone who is authorized by another (the principal) to act for or in place of the principal.

ANATOMICAL GIFT   An *anatomical gift* is the donation of all or part of the body of the decedent for the purpose of transplantation or research.

ANCILLARY ADMINISTRATION *Ancillary Administration* is a Probate proceeding that aids or assists the original (primary) Probate proceeding. Ancillary administration is conducted in another state to determine the beneficiary of the decedent's property located within that state.

ANNUAL GIFT TAX EXCLUSION The *Annual Gift Tax Exclusion* is the amount a person can gift to another each year without being required to file a federal Gift Tax Return. The Annual Gift Tax Exclusion is currently $11,000.

ANNUITANT An *annuitant* is someone who is entitled to receive payments under an annuity contract.

ANNUITY An *annuity* is the right to receive periodic payments (monthly, quarterly) for the life of the annuitant or for a given number of years.

ASSET An *asset* is anything owned by someone that has a value, including personal property (jewelry, paintings, securities, cash, motor vehicles, etc.) and real property (condominiums, vacant lots, acreage, residences, etc.)

BENEFICIARY A *beneficiary* is one who benefits from the act of another or from the transfer of property. In this book we refer to a beneficiary as someone named in a Will or Trust to receive property, or someone who inherits property under the Laws of Descent and Distribution.

BOND A *bond*, is a written document that guarantees the faithful performance of certain acts or duties (see Surety Bond)

CFR   *CFR* is the abbreviation for the *Code of Federal Regulations.*

CLAIM A *claim* against the decedent's Estate is a demand for payment. To be effective, the claim must be filed with the Probate court within the time limits set by law.

CODE A *Code* is a body of laws arranged systematically for easy reference e.g. the Internal Revenue Code.

COLUMBARIUM A *columbarium* is a vault with niches (spaces) for urns that contain the ashes of cremated bodies.

COMMISSIONER   A *Commissioner* is someone appointed by the Court or by the government to do a job.

COMMON LAW MARRIAGE   A *common law marriage* is one that is entered into without a state marriage license nor any kind of official marriage ceremony. A common law marriage is created by an agreement to marry, followed by the two living together as man and wife. Most states do not recognize a common law marriage as being a valid marriage.

CONFLICT OF INTEREST A *conflict of interest* is a conflict between the official duties of a fiduciary (Guardian, Trustee, attorney, etc.) and his own private interest. For example, it is a conflict of interest for a Successor Trustee to use Trust property for his own personal profit.

CONSERVATOR A *Conservator* is a person appointed by the Probate court to preserve and manage the property of a person who incapacitated.

CREDITOR A *creditor* is someone to whom a debt is owed by another person (the *debtor*).

CREMAINS The word *cremains* is an abbreviation of the term *cremated remains*. It is also referred to as the *ashes* of a person who has been cremated.

CUSTODIAN   A *Custodian* under the Massachusetts *Uniform Transfers to Minors Act* is a person or a financial institution that accepts responsibility for the care and management of property given to a minor child.

CURTESY **Curtesy** is the right of a husband, upon the death of his wife, to a Life Estate in real property she owned during their marriage, provided they had a surviving child who could inherit the property. This English Common Law has been abolished in most states, including Massachusetts, however, Massachusetts has a right of DOWER for the surviving spouse.

DAMAGES **Damages** is money that is awarded by a Court as compensation to someone who has been injured by the action of another.

DEBTOR A **debtor** is someone who owes payment of money or services to another person (the **creditor**).

DECEDENT The **decedent** is the person who died.

DESCENDANT A **descendant** is someone who descends from a common ancestor. There are two kinds of descendants: a **lineal descendant** and a **collateral descendant**. A lineal descendant is one who descends in a straight line such as father to son to grandson. The collateral descendant is one who descends in a parallel line, such as a cousin. In this book, unless otherwise stated, the term **descendant** refers to a **lineal descendant**.

DISTRIBUTION The **distribution** of a Trust Estate or of a Probate Estate is the transfer to a beneficiary that part of the Estate to which the beneficiary is entitled.

DISBURSE To **disburse** the Probate Estate is to use Probate funds to pay monies owed by the decedent or by the decedent's Estate.

DOWER *Dower* is the right of a wife, upon the death of her husband, to a Life Estate in one-third of all real property that he owned during their marriage. This English Common Law has been abolished in most states. Massachusetts has modified this Common Law to include rights for the husband and wife. Dower rights in Massachusetts are limited to a 1/3 Life Estate interest in real property owned by the deceased spouse at the time of his/her death

DURABLE POWER OF ATTORNEY A *Durable Power of Attorney* is a document in which the person who signs the document (the *Principal*) gives another person (his *Attorney in Fact*) authority to do certain things on behalf of the Principal. The Attorney in Fact is also referred to as the Principal's *Agent*. The word *"durable"* means that the authority of the Agent continues even if the Principal is incapacitated at the time that the Agent is acting on behalf of the Principal.

DURESS *Duress* is any unlawful threat or pressure used to force someone to act (or to refrain from acting) in a certain manner.

ESTATE A person's *Estate* is all of the property (both real and personal property) owned by that person. A person's Estate is also referred to as his *taxable estate* because all of the decedent's assets must be included when determining whether any Estate taxes are due when the person dies. Compare to *Probate Estate*.

ESTATE OF HOMESTEAD In Massachusetts, an *Estate of Homestead* is created, either by deed or by the filing of a Declaration of Homestead. Once established, up to $300,000 of the equity in the homestead is protected from the claims of creditors,

EXECUTOR An *Executor* is someone appointed by a Will maker to carry out the directions and requests in his Will.

FIDUCIARY A *Fiduciary* is one who takes on the duty of holding property in Trust for another or acting for the benefit of another, such as a Personal Representative, Trustee, Guardian etc.. A fiduciary relationship is also one that is developed out of trust and confidence. For example, an attorney has a fiduciary relationship with his client.

GRANTEE The *Grantee* named in a deed is the person who receives title to the property from the grantor.

GRANTOR A *Grantor* is someone who transfers property. The grantor of a deed, (also called the party of the first part), is the person who transfers property to a new owner (the *Grantee*). The grantor of a Trust is someone who creates the Trust and then transfers property into the Trust. Also see *Settlor*.

HEALTH CARE AGENT A *Health Care Agent* is someone who is appointed under a Health Care Power of Attorney to make medical decisions for another (the *Principal)* in the event that the Principal is too ill to make those decisions for himself.

HEALTH CARE PROXY A *Health Care Proxy* is a written document in which someone (the *Principal*) appoints another (his *Health Care Agent*) to make health care decisions on behalf of the Principal in the event that the Principal is too sick to make such decisions.

HEIR An *heir* is anyone entitled to inherit the decedent's property under the Laws of Descent and Distribution in the event that the decedent dies without a Will.

INDIGENT   An person who is *indigent* is one who is poor, destitute and without funds.

INCAPACITATED   The term *incapacitated* is used in two ways. A person is *physically incapacitated* if he lacks the ability to care for himself in some way. A person is *legally incapacitated* if a court finds that a person is unable to care for his person or property. Once the Court determines that a person is legally incapacitated, the judge will appoint someone to care for person or property of the incapacitated person.

INTER VIVOS TRUST   An *Inter Vivos Trust* (also known as a *Living Trust*) is Trust that is created and becomes effective during the lifetime of the Grantor (or Settlor) as opposed to a Trust that he includes as part of his Will to take effect upon his death.

INTESTATE   *Intestate* means not having a Will or dying without a Will. *Testate* is to have a Will or dying with a Will.

IRREVOCABLE CONTRACT   An *irrevocable* contract is a contract that cannot be revoked, withdrawn, or cancelled by any of the parties to that contract.

JOINT TENANCY   In Massachusetts, a *Joint Tenancy* means that each of tenant owns an equal share of the property with right of survivorship; i.e., should one Joint Tenant die the remaining tenants own the property.

JOINT AND SEVERAL LIABILITY   If two or more people agree to be *jointly and severally liable* to pay the debt, then that means that each agree individually to be responsible to pay for the debt, and together they all agree to pay for the debt.

KEY MAN INSURANCE   *Key man insurance* is an insurance policy designed to protect a company from economic loss in the event that an important employee of the company becomes disabled or dies.

KINDRED   *Kindred* are those related by blood. They are also referred to as *Kinsfolk*.

LEGALESE *Legalese* is the special vocabulary used by attorneys to draft legal documents. Many consider legalese to be unnecessarily complex and incomprehensible.

LETTERS   *Letters* refers to a document, issued by the Probate court, giving the person who is appointed as Personal Representative, authority to take settle the decedent's Estate.

LIEN   A *Lien* is a charge or a claim on someone's property as security for a debt. If the debt is not paid, the lender can take legal action to get possession of the property as payment for the debt.

LIFE ESTATE   A *Life Estate* interest in real property is the right to possess and occupy the property for so long as the owner of the Life Estate lives. When the owner of the Life Estate dies, the property will belong to the owner of the *Remainder Interest*.

LITIGATION   *Litigation* is the process of carrying on a lawsuit, i.e., to sue for some right or remedy in a court of law. A Litigation Attorney is one who is experienced in conducting the law suit and in particular, going to trial.

MEDICAID *Medicaid* is a public assistance program sponsored jointly by the federal and state government to provide medical care for people with few assets and low income.

MGL   *MGL* is the abbreviation for the ***Massachusetts General Laws***.

NEXT OF KIN   ***Next of kin*** has two meanings in law: it can refer to a person's nearest blood relation or it can refer to those people (not necessarily blood relations) who are entitled to inherit the property of the decedent if the decedent died without a Will.

NON-PROBATE TRANSFER A ***Non-probate Transfer*** is the transfer of property to the decedent's beneficiary without the necessity of a Probate Procedure. This includes property that is transferred to the surviving joint owner, or property transferred to the beneficiary of a Pay-On-Death accounts.

PERJURY ***Perjury*** is lying under oath. The false statement can be made as a witness in court or by signing an Affidavit. Perjury is a criminal offense.

PERSONAL EFFECTS ***Personal effects*** is personal property that is kept for one's personal use such as clothing, jewelry, books, and other items generally found in the home.

PERSONAL PROPERTY ***Personal property*** is all property owned by a person that is not real property (real estate). It includes personal effects, cars, securities, bank accounts, insurance policies, etc.

PERSONAL REPRESENTATIVE   The ***Personal Representative*** is someone (the Administrator or Executor) appointed by the Probate court to settle the decedent's Estate and to distribute whatever is left to the proper beneficiary.

PETITION A ***Petition*** is a formal written request to a Court asking the Court to take action or issue an order on a given matter.

POSTNUPTIAL AGREEMENT A *Postnuptial Agreement* is an agreement made by a couple after marriage to decide their respective rights in the event of a divorce or the death of a spouse.

PRENUPTIAL AGREEMENT A *prenuptial agreement* (also known as an *antenuptial agreement*) is an agreement made prior to marriage whereby a couple determines how their property is to be managed during their marriage and how their property is to be divided should one die, or they later divorce.

PROBATE *Probate* is a Court procedure in which a Court determines the existence of a valid Will. The Decedent's Estate is then settled by the Personal Representative who pays all valid claims and then distributes whatever remains to the proper beneficiary.

PROBATE ESTATE The *Probate Estate* is that part of the decedent's Estate that is subject to Probate. It includes property that the decedent owned in his name only. It does not include property that was jointly held by the decedent and another. It does not include property held "in Trust for" or "for the benefit of" someone.

REAL PROPERTY *Real property,* also known as *real estate,* is land and anything permanently attached to the land such as buildings and fences.

RECEIVER A *Receiver* is a person appointed by the court to preserve property when there is a pending court procedure and there is danger that the property may be lost, removed or injured, before the matter is resolved. For example, the Probate Court will appoint a Receiver to care for the property of someone who is missing.

REMAINDER INTEREST See LIFE ESTATE

REPARATION   *Reparation* is money paid to make up for an injury or wrongdoing.

RESIDUARY BENEFICIARY A *residuary beneficiary* of a Will is a beneficiary who is entitled to whatever is left of the Probate Estate once the specific gifts made in the Will have been distributed and once the decedent's bills, taxes and costs of Probate have been paid. If there is more than one residuary beneficiary, then they share equally in the residuary Estate, unless the Will provides for a different distribution.

RESIDUARY ESTATE A *Residuary Estate* is that part of a Probate Estate that is left after all expenses and costs of administration have been paid and specific gifts have been distributed.

REVOCABLE TRUST   A *Revocable Trust* is a Trust which can be amended or revoked by the Grantor or Settlor during his lifetime.

REVOCABLE LIVING TRUST A *Revocable Living Trust* (also known as an *Inter Vivos Trust*) is a Revocable Trust that is created and becomes effective during the lifetime of the Grantor or Settlor.

RIGHT OF REPRESENTATION   If a group of people inherit a gift with a *Right of Representation*, then should one of the group die before the gift is given, then the deceased person's share goes to his/her lineal descendants. If the decedent died without descendants, then the share is distributed to the surviving members of the group.

SETTLOR   A *Settlor* or *Trustor* is someone who creates a Trust.

SIBLING   A *sibling* is one of two or more people born of the same parents; i.e., a brother or a sister. Unless, otherwise noted, we used the term to include those who have only one parent in common; i.e. a half brother or a half sister.

SOLEMNIZE   To *solemnize* a marriage is to enter a marriage publicly, before witnesses, rather than privately as in a common law marriage.

SPECIFIC GIFT)   A *Specific Gift* is a gift of a specific item, or part of the Will maker's Estate, that is made to a named beneficiary of the Will.

SPENDTHRIFT   A *spendthrift* is someone who wastes money and/or spends lavishly.

SPENDTHRIFT TRUST   A *Spendthrift Trust* is a Trust created to provide monies to a beneficiary, and at the same time protect the Trust property from being taken by the creditors of the beneficiary.

STATUTE OF LIMITATION   A *Statute of Limitation* is a federal or state law that sets maximum time periods for taking legal action. Once the time set out in the statute passes, no legal action can be taken.

STEPPED-UP BASIS   A *stepped-up basis* is the value placed on property that is acquired in a taxable transaction such as inheriting property or purchasing property (Internal Revenue Code 1012). The "step-up" refers to the increase in value from the basis of the former owner (usually what he paid for it), to the basis of the new owner (usually the market value when the transfer is made).

SURETY BOND   A *surety bond* (as used in this book) is a bond issued by an insurance company that guarantees payment for a loss suffered because the Personal Representative failed to do his job properly.

SUCCESSOR TRUSTEE   A *Successor Trustee* is someone who takes the place of the Trustee.

TENANCY BY THE ENTIRETY A *Tenancy by the Entirety* is the name of a form of ownership of real property held by a husband and wife. It is a joint tenancy with right of survivorship, modified by the common law theory that the husband and wife are one.

TENANCY IN COMMON   *Tenancy In Common* is a form of ownership such that each tenant owns his/her share without any claim to that share by the other tenants. There is no right of survivorship. Once a Tenant In Common dies, his share belongs to the tenant's Estate.

TESTATE   *Testate* means having a Will or dying with a Will.

TITLE INSURANCE   *Title Insurance* is a policy issued by a title company after searching title to the property. The insurance covers losses that result from a defect of title, such as unpaid taxes, or someone with a claim of ownership of the property.

TRUST AGREEMENT A *Trust agreement* is document in which someone (the Grantor or Settlor) creates a Trust and appoints a Trustee to manage property placed into the Trust. The usual purpose of the Trust is to benefit persons or charities named by the Grantor as beneficiaries of the Trust.

TRUSTEE   A *Trustee* is a person, or institution, who accepts the
duty of caring for property for the benefit of another.

UNDUE INFLUENCE *Undue influence* is pressure or persuasion
that overpowers a person's free will so that the dominated person is not acting intelligently or voluntarily.

WAIVER   A *waiver* is the intentional and voluntary giving up of
a known right.

WARRANTY DEED   A *Warranty Deed* is a deed in which the
Grantor warrants (promises) that the property he is
transferring has good and clear title; i.e., that no one
else has rights in the property. This is different than a
Quit-claim Deed where the Grantor says, in effect, "I
am releasing any interest I have in this property to you,
but I make no guarantees about anyone else's right to
this property."

WRONGFUL DEATH   A *wrongful death* is a death that was
caused by the willful or negligent act of a person
or company.

INDEX

WEB SITES

MASSACHUSETTS WEB SITES

150 Massachusetts Statutes are referenced in
Guiding Those Left Behind In Massachusetts

Each state has its own set of laws relating to the settlement of a person's Estate. The laws that are referenced in this book are very different from the laws of other states.

The author is in now in the process of "translating"
Guiding Those Left Behind
for the rest of the states, that is, writing state specific books that explain how to settle the affairs of someone who dies in the given state.

The following states are now in print:
ALABAMA, ARIZONA, CALIFORNIA, CONNECTICUT
FLORIDA, GEORGIA, HAWAII, ILLINOIS, INDIANA. IOWA
KENTUCKY, LOUISIANA, MASSACHUSETTS, MARYLAND
MICHIGAN, MINNESOTA, MISSOURI, MISSISSIPPI
NEW JERSEY, NEW YORK, NORTH CAROLINA, OHIO
PENNSYLVANIA, SOUTH CAROLINA, TENNESSEE
TEXAS, VIRGINIA, WASHINGTON, WISCONSIN

Readers of this book can purchase *Guiding Those Left Behind* for $22. This includes shipping.

To order or to check for book availability in other states call Eagle Publishing Company at (800) 824-0823.
- or -
Visit our Web site http://www.eaglepublishing.com

BOOK REVIEWS OF *Guiding Those Left Behind*

ARIZONA
Ben T. Traywick of the Tombstone Epitaph said "This book is an excellent reference book that simplifies all the necessary tasks that must be done when there is a death in the family. There is even an explanation as to how you can arrange your own estate so that your heirs will not be left with a multitude of nagging problems." "The reviewer has been going through probate for two years with no end yet in sight. This book at the beginning two year ago would have helped immensely."

CALIFORNIA
Margot Petit Nichols of the Carmel Pine Cone called it a ". . .TRULY RIVETING READ." " . . . I could scarcely put it down." "This is a book that we should all have, either on our book shelves or thoughtfully placed with our important papers."

FLORIDA
Maryhelen Clague of the Tampa Tribune Times wrote "Amelia Pohl has created a handy, self-help guide that illustrates the necessary steps that must be taken when someone dies, a guide that is easy to read, extremely clear and simple to refer to when the need arises."

NEW YORK
Saul Friedman of NEWSDAY said "And one section that should be read by readers of any age, suggests and describes how to create an 'If I Die' file to point the way to your vital papers and policies, to minimize the problems and costs for your survivors. Alas, not even you boomers will live forever."

Beyond Grief To Acceptance and Peace

AMELIA E. POHL and the noted psychologist BARBARA J. SIMMONDS, Ph.d, have written a book for those families who have suffered a loss.

Beyond Grief To Acceptance and Peace explains:
- ◇ What to say to the bereaved
- ◇ How to help a child through the loss
- ◇ Strategies to adjust to a new lifestyle
- ◇ When and where to seek assistance.

The second edition of this 80 page book is now available for $10.95 plus shipping and handling. You can order the book using the following discount coupon for a total of $10.

DISCOUNT COUPON

Please send me a copy of Beyond Grief To Acceptance and Peace

☐ I am enclosing a check for $10.
☐ Charge this to my _____ credit card
　　　　　　　　　　(Visa, Master, Discover)
Credit Card no. _____

Expiration date: _____

Name _____

Address _____

_____

Mail this coupon to:
　　EAGLE PUBLISHING COMPANY OF BOCA
　　　　4199 N. Dixie Hwy. #2
　　　　Boca Raton, FL 33431

A Will is Not Enough

Many people who have a Will think that they have their affairs in order. They believe that their Will can take care of any problem that may arise. But the primary function of a Will it to distribute property to people named in a Will. A Will cannot:

⇨ Protect your assets and limit your debt

⇨ Provide care for a minor or disabled child

⇨ Avoid Guardianship

⇨ Appoint someone to make your health care decisions should you be unable to do so

⇨ Appoint someone to handle your finances should you be unable to do so

⇨ Arrange to pay for your health care should you need long term nursing care, including qualifying for MEDICAID.

AMELIA E. POHL, Esq. has written a series of state specific books explaining how to do all of these things. This new book series is a continuation of this book. It builds on basic Estate Planning concepts introduced in Chapter 7 of this book and then goes on to introduce other, more sophisticated, Estate Planning methods. Although the topics are sophisticated, the writing style is the same as in this book. It is written in plain English. It is intended for use by the average person.

A Will Is Not Enough is now available for:

ARIZONA, CALIFORNIA, CONNECTICUT, FLORIDA
GEORGIA, HAWAII, INDIANA, MARYLAND
MASSACHUSETTS, MICHIGAN, NEBRASKA, NEW JERSEY
NEW MEXICO, NEW YORK, OREGON, PENNSYLVANIA
TEXAS, VIRGINIA, WASHINGTON, WISCONSIN

Readers of this book can purchase *A Will Is Not Enough* for $25. To check for book availability in other states call Eagle Publishing Company at (800) 824-0823.

It is the goal of EAGLE PUBLISHING COMPANY to keep our publications fresh.

As we receive information about changes to the federal or state law we will post an update to this edition at our Web site.

http://www.eaglepublishing.com